WITHDRAWN

Crosscurrents / MODERN CRITIQUES

Harry T. Moore, *General Editor*

REBECCA WEST
Artist and Thinker

Peter Wolfe

WITH A PREFACE BY
Harry T. Moore

SOUTHERN ILLINOIS UNIVERSITY PRESS
Carbondale and Edwardsville

FEFFER & SIMONS, INC.
London and Amsterdam

To some patient friends who taught me to love books

Marvin Magalaner
Arthur Schwartz
Milton Slocum
Carl Strauch
Paul Wiley

Copyright © 1971, by Southern Illinois University Press
All rights reserved
Printed in the United States of America
Designed by Andor Braun
ISBN 0-8093-0483-X
Library of Congress Catalog Card Number 73-132486

Contents

Preface

It is good, and it is useful, to have a book about the writing of Rebecca West. She has generally been discussed only in reviews. Since her own first book (on Henry James in 1916, the year of his death), she has become widely known as a superior reporter and less known as a middle-group novelist. The "superior reporter" term may do her an injustice, for her books of nonfiction deserve better than faint praise. The somewhat encyclopedic Twentieth-Century Authors, in its first supplement in 1955, says she is known as "the foremost woman journalist of Great Britain and the United States," but even this seems to be a rather weak statement of her position. In her particular area, travelogues, literary criticism, and treason trials, what male journalist is better? The only ones who can be immediately invoked are James Morris and Gerald Brenan, both Englishmen and not really "better"; a writer such as John Gunther, for all his sharpness of observation, never penetrated the depths of this terrain as Rebecca West and the two Englishmen have.

She is herself of Irish birth, into an Anglo-Irish family. Her mother was Scottish, and the young Rebecca West was brought up and educated in Edinburgh. In her youth she became an actress, but soon tired of that occupation, though it at least gave Cecily Isabel Fairfield the name she uses in her writing. She had played Rebecca West in Ibsen's Rosmersholm.

She once wrote me a pleasant letter—out of the blue, as the phrase goes. She had read something I had written about D. H. Lawrence and kindly gave me some information which

I didn't use in The Life and Works of D. H. Lawrence because *I* had regrettably mislaid her letter. Not long afterward the book was reviewed anonymously in the Times Literary Supplement (London), which spoke of the book in a friendly way, but found one fault with it: it didn't use the material which Miss West (or Dame Rebecca, as she is now) had provided me with. So I discerned, through the fog of TLS anonymity, the identity of the reviewer. One could only feel deeply honored. About fifteen years later I saw her at a party in London at Lady Audley's (no, not the Lady Audley of the secret), but didn't meet Dame Rebecca and was too timid to approach and offer a self-introduction, or even to ask Lady Audley to "present" me. But it was interesting just to see Rebecca West, with her sharp bright eyes.

These are the eyes that have looked so deeply into many important phases of modern life. It seems to me that, in the present book, Peter Wolfe somewhat underrates Rebecca West as a novelist, though his criticism, for the most part technical, is sound enough. He does make some important points here. I characterized her, above, as "a middle-group novelist," meaning that she was difficult to "place." Surely those of us who have read her novels have been delighted with them, despite the defects Mr. Wolfe speaks of. These novels have a wonderful quality of life and brightness; one remembers them long after one has read them, while the work of many writers of fiction fades out of the mind. I can recall the early novels and feel that the latest one, The Birds Fall Down (1966), is exceptionally good. Mr. Wolfe rightly calls it her "boldest fiction," using "the form of the thriller to make a serious moral statement"—a dramatization of the madness of our world as well as an "attempt to restore a religious intensity to life"—and Mr. Wolfe draws comparisons between The Birds Fall Down and Conrad's The Secret Agent. And of course both of them project the anxieties of espionage and are richly atmospheric, Conrad's book set in London and Rebecca West's in London and in Paris (the Étoile area).

Mr. Wolfe gives most of his attention to Rebecca West's prose writings—which are not at all prosy. She is a rhythmic and vivid writer with a finely sharpened intelligence. In discussing her volume of criticism, The Court and the Castle, Mr. Wolfe points out that this valuable contribution to Shakespeareology links Rebecca West's social and literary interests in a way that none of her other books do. In passing, Mr. Wolfe mentions the undeserved neglect of another book which, like The Court and the Castle, is the result of a lifetime's reading: J. B. Priestley's Literature and Western Man. Even those of us who consider Mr. Priestley's novels hopelessly bound to the outmoded and his plays not much above the ordinary can appreciate his book on world literature: similarly, anyone under the spell of Shakespeare can appreciate Dame Rebecca's book, which Mr. Wolfe deals with at some length, without noting, however, that her view of Hamlet as being decisive (what we would at this moment call activist) rather than irresolute was a theory which A. C. Bradley was the first critic writing in English to make use of.

Saving one of his favorites for an orchestrated conclusion, Peter Wolfe writes with great enthusiasm about Rebecca West's Black Lamb and Grey Falcon, which earlier in the book he had spoken of as "the masterpiece of travel literature in our century"; but surely there are a few other volumes which can stand with it, for example Henry James's The American Scene, D. H. Lawrence's Sea and Sardinia, or even Norman Douglas's Old Calabria and some of the work of the previously mentioned James Morris and Gerald Brenan. But even to speak of these books and writers in connection with Black Lamb and Grey Falcon is to give that volume a boost upward. It is certainly one of the masterworks among travel books in our time. And it gives Mr. Wolfe a strong ending for his critical study which, once again, it is good to have, for in itself it is excellent, and also necessary.

HARRY T. MOORE

Southern Illinois University
October 25, 1970

Acknowledgments

The time and energy of many people went into the writing of this book. I want to thank, first of all, Mr. and Mrs. G. Evelyn Hutchinson for their friendly encouragement; Marjorie Wynne of Yale University's Beinecke Library for putting me in touch with important materials concerning the book; John Onuska for his help with important background data; Don Crinklaw, Jane Parks, and James Tierney for helping me with matters of organization and style; Audria Shumard for typing the manuscript; and the University of Missouri–St. Louis Research Council for grants to cover expenses connected with the manuscript's preparation.

The combined help of the following people amounts to a major contribution: Virgil Sands, Jill Auerbach, Guido Kneitel, Robert Degenhardt, Heidi Reichmann, Annette Cohen, Richard T. Springmeyer, Verlin Wheeler, Richard Graham, and Paula Kimmel.

The author and publisher join in expressing their thanks to the Yale University Press for permission to quote passages from G. E. Hutchinson's *The Itinerant Ivory Tower: Scientific and Literary Essays* and from Rebecca West's *The Court and the Castle: Some Treatments of a Recurrent Theme.* Grateful appreciation is extended to Dame Rebecca West and her agent, A. D. Peters, for permission to quote from the works of Rebecca West which she controls. Appreciation is also extended to the Viking Press, Inc., for permission to quote from the following works of Rebecca West: *The Thinking Reed, Black Lamb and Grey Falcon: A Journey through Yugoslavia, A Train of Powder* (which originally appeared in the *New Yorker*), *The New Meaning of Treason, The Fountain Overflows,* and *The Birds Fall Down.*

Rebecca West
Artist and Thinker

1

The Wheel

Rebecca West's literary career is outstanding both in scope and durability. She began writing reviews at age nineteen for *Freewoman*; the following year (1912) she joined *Clarion* as a political writer and has continued to write for British and American periodicals. Setting aside her hundred-odd early magazine pieces, the interval between her first and most recent book spans fifty years. Her output during this busy career is richly varied: political journalism, literary criticism, biography, history, travel sketches, and fiction.

If this vast and varied output holds together, the unifying core must be the Augustinian doctrine of original sin. An effect, argued Augustine, cannot be greater than its cause. If we are nothing ourselves—not good or bad, but nothing —none of our strivings can have any reality. Although she has written an interpretive biography of St. Augustine (1933), she has never exorcised him. Her books continue to insist that there is more evil than good in our world and that the evil is more vivid. Man's depravity energizes the two myths symbolically designated in the title, *Black Lamb and Grey Falcon* (1941). It undergirds Rebecca West's distrust of the worldliness usually equated with the male principle. It saturates her reading of Shakespeare: the palace intrigues in the histories and tragedies show what happens when the will acts in a milieu where the will counts as nothing; *The Court and the Castle* (1953) claims that Calvin, who insures the salvation of a few, sparkles and glints sunshine next to Shakespeare, who damns all. Rebecca West's own characters seem determined by what they *are*, not by what they do. Their choices do not create new opportunities. Alice Pemberton, of "The Salt of the Earth" (1934), does evil things in order to punish herself for a nonspecifiable crime. This self-destructiveness, all the stronger for its involuntary nature, recurs in Rebecca West's criticism. Here is her reading of Kipling:

> He stands among those . . . who . . . are treading the road to the highest honours, when they are assailed by passions, which seem not to be a part of the victim's individualities, but to have crawled out of the dark uncharted sea of our common humanity.

Her reading of Augustine reflects the same dark urgency:

> He had an excessive share of that feeling of guilt which exists quite unrelated to any individual experience in the mind of almost every human being. It seemed to him as if humanity was saturated with the obscene, not by reason of what it did but of what it was.[1]

The driving spirit both of modern life and Rebecca West is not Marx or Freud, but the cruel, guilt-ridden African monk whose disgust with human flesh kept him from loving anything other than an odorless, disembodied spirit: "Every phrase I read of his [Augustine] sounds in my ears like the sentence of my doom and the doom of my age." [2]

This Augustinian streak has apparently not jaded her zest for life. On the contrary, our exertions build the bone and muscle which fights the darkness. Suitably, the authors she has discussed at greatest length—Shakespeare, James, Bennett, Lawrence—have been the most industrious and devoted. Her pessimism is qualified by her toughness. But beyond her admiration of bravery, courage, and endurance we cannot go. Her Augustinian streak is too elusive. Were it deeper and ruddier, she would not ponder subjects like justice and religion. Were she less stained by the streak, it would be no sticking point. At times the streak is faint; at other times she seems to have erased it completely, as in *The Thinking Reed* (1936), where the clumsy doer wins the beautiful girl. Then it recurs in her next book, *Black*

Lamb and Grey Falcon, where it pollutes the Habsburg dynasty, Western Europe's attitude toward the Balkan peninsula, and British foreign policy in the 1930s. There is something primordial about these recurrences. They are too shifting and complex to give themselves up to a systematic reading. The most we can do is to use Augustinian doctrine as a loose working frame for Rebecca West's conservative skepticism. She cannot escape the corrosive ooze of original sin. She sees all human values imperiled by this primordial stuff, whose harshest manifestation is a destructive rage that smashes anything capable of being smashed, including the self. It is no wonder that the citadel of Rebecca West's thought lacks a pleasing contour. The first movers of our consciousness are neither rational nor explainable by rational techniques. The ooze corrodes not only the bedrock on which the citadel stands, but also the bricks and mortar out of which the citadel is made:

> Primitive ideas may at any time reappear and throw out of gear the apparatus that has been so painfully adapted to civilized uses.

> Man does not want to know. When he knows very little he plays with the possibility of knowledge, but when he finds that the pieces he has been putting together are going to spell out the answer to the riddle he is frightened, and he throws them in every direction; and another civilization falls.[3]

If these deep-driving energies meet so little resistance, it is because our basic values are askew. In a 1937 essay on Elizabeth Montagu, Rebecca West mentions "that irrational disposition of humanity"[4] to favor unpleasant people while ignoring, sometimes even disliking, the gentle and loving. *The Thinking Reed* posits rudeness as the hallmark of the carriage trade. But the satire is double-edged. Although the chic internationals enjoy rebuffing their social inferiors, their rudeness only explains half the story. For their inferiors both expect and welcome abuse. Tradition dictates high-handedness as a rule in the game of social climbing. An aristocrat with good manners is no prize for the socially ambitious in Rebecca West. Any gain, to be certifiable as a gain, must carry with it a corresponding loss. This masochistic strain informs not only social class but also economics and politics. Farmers, who satisfy man's greatest need, have rarely been honored by western nations. *The Modern Rake's Progress* (1934), a morality for the Depression illustrated by David Low, makes the point that growing a nation's food counts less socially than manufacturing its mascara. George, the scion of an impoverished family of farmers, toils for two pounds a week as a clerk. A distant millionaire relative, the mascara mogul, is accidentally killed in a Chicago gang war and leaves his money to George, whereupon George becomes the Modern Rake. Again Rebecca West's satire is twin-barbed: while George is degrading himself, he is also serving the degrading inequities of our economy.

The universal human preference for the unpleasant over the pleasant enlarges to the sphere of religion in *Black Lamb and Grey Falcon*. Not only Augustine, but Paul, Luther, and the Mithraic cultists promoted ugliness and cruelty. Their preference is expressed in the contrast between the worship practices of eastern and western Christian sects. The eastern Christians conceive life as rich and round, something to be enjoyed. Their religion is an occasion to lavish abundance on themselves. This mode of life is cheerfully additive, glorying in opportunities to add good things to life. We westerners, however, aim to improve life by subtraction, not addition. We elevate loss, together with its companion, pain, to a category of faith:

> The worshippers in Western countries come before the altar with the desire to subtract from the godhead and themselves; to subtract benefits from the godhead by prayer, to subtract their dangerous adult qualities by affecting childishness.[5]

This debasement of religion is no mere outcropping of western capitalism. We feel driven to degrade ourselves in compensation for gaining something because we neither trust nor like ourselves. Rebecca West traces this disturbing trait to a restlessness that is more western than eastern. The tendency to migrate or colonize, a tendency more popular in mobile, mechanized societies, weakens cultural roots. The boyish twitch for roving and rough conquest carries with it a contempt for nontangible, nonnegotiable values. Our rootlessness creates instability and disorder. Patrick Braybrooke, one of Rebecca West's earliest critics, acknowledges his subject's probing pessimism. His disclaimer that the pessimism is unbalanced and arbitrary, however, is wrong:

> Probably because she can probe so deeply into human conduct is a reason that makes Miss West rather angry with humanity. . . . The mistake that Miss West seems to make is that she sees the bad side of humanity and fails to see the other.[6]

Braybrooke exaggerates. Profundity and pessimism need not be enmeshed. Secondly, neither Rebecca West nor humanity at large is so committed to despair. Here is her most concise statement on the subject of death; it comes from her 1931 feminist essay, "Woman as Artist and Thinker":

> The organism has indeed an inveterate tendency to live; hence certainly the will to live. But the organism has also an inveterate tendency to die. Take an X-ray photograph of a child of ten and you will see the white lines where already decay has begun to establish itself; it gains everywhere, it gains every day, and the mind has a profound sympathy with it, since it envisages death as a sensationless peace like that which it knew in the womb.[7]

Death's fascination is borne out by religious art. Over the centuries, death—not only Christ's—has inspired some of art's finest moments. Nor can the fascination be contained. The beautiful workmanship on tombs and sarcophagi, like our best elegies, transmits power to everybody. But instead of yielding to this power, Rebecca West makes the power work for life. If man includes within himself the will to live and the will to die, an awareness of death can teach us to coexist with danger—to deal with it wisely and thus turn it to our advantage. This adaptive function, while curbing cheap optimism, civilizes us. Once we distinguish true courage from romantic posturing, we dignify our actions. Our view of life's preciousness deepens, and we evolve the courage to maintain that preciousness without taking silly risks. Death and life are interwoven. An appreciation of the one entails a cool, steady look at the other.

The universe, then, is an uneasy mixture of good and bad. But Rebecca West does not immobilize herself; she leagues strenuously with the forces of order and wholeness. These forces compel our support, she argues, because they defy the general tendency to inertia. Her attitude is one of tough-minded relativism. The ability of the moral will to rouse supporters over the centuries proves the imperishability of transcendent ideals. Although it never thrives like its opposite, order is as real as disorder. Sensibly, Rebecca West takes it in whatever form she can. Not to do so would be a denial both of life and of the forces that best perpetuate life. Her accounts of war-torn Europe in 1946–47 are full of bureaucratic blunders, communication failures, and supply shortages. These postwar essays, though, do not attack democracy. They discuss democratic techniques of postwar reconstruction. So long as Europe's economy was staggering, controls had to be imposed, often rigorously. Deeply unhappy with the discomfort and the sheer nastiness these controls bring, she sees no feasible alternative to them. Rebecca West cherishes justice so much that she wishes it more effective and more equable: only a just society will externalize health and happiness as social goals. Yet she never dissolves the problem of justice in party politics, mystical certainties, or sentimental wish-projections. She bases her decision to retain controls on a spectrum of contingencies, not all of which are political or economic:

> It was necessary to have all these controls because Hitler had made us bankrupt. We could not let people import what they fancied from America. . . . If we sacked the Labor government tomorrow, the re-entering Tories could not abolish controls. But how could there be controls without controllers who did not . . . human nature being as beastely as it is . . . enjoy the mean pleasure of refusal? [8]

Rebecca West's best critic, G. E. Hutchinson, sees his subject as both tragic and comic:

> If the universe appears to lack love, to be devoid of sweet-
> ness, we must invent love and sweetness. . . . Rebecca
> West's books are full of good food, music and dancing, of
> the delights of the mind and a connoisseur's appreciation
> of human individuality.[9]

As with the law, we must foster whatever love and sweetness
we invent. Life can only thrive in a climate of happiness.
Renunciation imposes the burden of loss; pain, while failing
to purify sin, prolongs sin; sacrifice is a rite that drips with
the blood of centuries. Rebecca West cheerfully advises us
to pursue pleasure. Her advice is no shoulder-shrugging denial of moral responsibility. While pleasure abets the life-
giving harmony between an organism and its environment,
it is hard work. The pleasure-seeker has to be original, self-
confident, and compassionate. It is much easier to court pain.
Thus the pleasure principle builds moral fiber. To protect the
sacredness of joy, we must repress the hatred and cruelty in-
grained in all of us and encourage others to do the same. The
streak, on the other hand, has accident, the law, and religion
doing its sick work. It requires much less watchfulness.

Rebecca West's urge to order drives her to concepts. To
invent love and sweetness is not enough. One must translate
love and sweetness into sharable social principles, an unend-
ing task that brings a note of existentialism to Rebecca
West's thought: "The sum will not add up. It is madness to
rack our brains over the sum. But there is nothing else we can
do except try to add up this sum." [10] The sum adds best in
the presence of love. Love is the supreme authority and measure. Like culture and tradition, it blocks harshness and promotes happiness. Yet it is not a progressive integration.
When it happens it defies causality. Its totem in Rebecca
West's early fiction is the hawthorn, a thorny shrub whose
flowers bloom with near-miraculous speed. Like this sudden
emergence of beauty, love has the lyricism of a spiritual revelation or epiphany. Its deepest manifestation occurs in the
worship service of the Eastern Church. Divine love excludes

nobody: no distinctions or gradations obtain. Rich and poor, young and old, criminal and lawman, stand together in the same part of the church to receive God's equal blessing. Secular love has some of this metaphysical dynamism. It too blesses whatever it touches, erasing differences of age, rank, and culture. Places where love is affirmed become magically charged in Rebecca West's fiction; but most of all, the enchantment transfigures the persons involved. The new identity is not primarily sexual. Sex is minor in Rebecca West. She ranges sex together with drinking as drives that most people keep within civilized bounds. (Incest, especially, owing to its low incidence outside the uneducated classes, she sees vastly overrated as a social menace.) The characters who love and are loved feel better, work better, and enjoy life more fully than the ones who have nobody. If they also lust more avidly, as they do in *The Thinking Reed*, it is a function of their richer, livelier response to stimuli in general.

Like the other energies that serve life, love does not sustain itself automatically. It needs constant trimming and refurbishing. For even in a healthy, thriving state, it can do the uncivilizing work of its opposite. European history contains many cruelties performed in love's name. Characters in Rebecca West's novels often use love as a whip to punish the ones who care for them. Rebecca West's love ethic stresses invisibility and selflessness. Love should ask nothing. Most of all, it should not trespass upon the things people live by, even if these things are lies. Yet caution and restraint do not always hold good. For love bruises by neglect just as easily as by clutching its object too tightly. The three passages quoted below point up the ridicule, the agony, and the skimpy returns often involved in loving. Love, then, blurs with the streak. But again, Rebecca West accepts the impure mixture because love comes in no other form:

> It is part of the martyrdom of his love [that of Bloom in Joyce's *Ulysses*] that it might be done clownishly, with no upgrowth into dignity, squatting and snuffing.

> There was nothing to do in this world except to love, but that had to be done with prudence carried to a degree that amounted to agony.

That is just what I cannot bear . . . that we should love each other and should act as enemies.[11]

The trimming and refurbishing of love is done better by women than by men. This is the core of Rebecca West's feminism. Braybrooke reports the writer to have said in "a morning journal": "I like to see men in a subordinate position, that is all they are fit for." [12] Such a remark is out of character. She neither praises women nor attacks men without qualification; even the early feminist novel, *The Judge* (1922), pokes mild fun at its suffragette heroine. Rebecca West grounds her feminism in natural process. Indulging a tendency to analogize from science, she makes female love a biological necessity. Survival itself impinges upon the maternal instinct. Women contain the seed of life; they can love and protect this precious seed to their last breath without ever having heard, seen, or touched it. Men cannot equal this commitment to unrevealed, uncreated life. And nothing male can match the physical and psychical joy women experience in childbirth. Whereas women thrive on generation, men are threatened by it. The shorter life-span of men spells out the firmer stand the female principle takes alongside life.

The roving acquisitive male seeks meaning outside the self, usually in a measurable commodity or else in an honor or title negotiable as cash, status, or property.

Men lack all sense of objective reality and have a purely pragmatic attitude to knowledge. A fact does not begin to be for a man until he has calculated its probable usefulness to him. . . . This means that he is not sure of the existence of his own soul, for nothing is more debatable for any of us than whether it is a good or a bad thing that our souls should have come to be.[13]

Ironically, then, the roving male has a much narrower frame than his homebody mate. Instead of strengthening the fiber of life from within, he weakens it by piling on gewgaws. His values are superficial, not organic. His opportunism weakens the magnetic circuit between himself and the coil of forces that shaped him. He fears beauty because of its incalculabil-

ity. Lacking the requisites for self-knowledge and self-acceptance, he has no stable basis upon which to build a personality.

Having willfully cut himself from so many rich sources of
meaning, he certifies his existence by mistreating women.
Rebecca West calls this predatory male need for assurances
"infantilism." Sexually it takes the form of physical conquest
followed by disavowal. The program gratifies both man's lust
and his sense of social solidarity. Distrustful of himself, he
neither loves nor trusts anyone who gives him pleasure. His
failure to make a deep commitment grounded in sex sends
him outdoors, where he huddles noisily with his friends
around the campfire of accepted social canons. So while the
peasant works his mate to death, the aristocrat uses her as a
pawn in political diplomacy.

Black Lamb and Grey Falcon labels the male defect
"lunacy," a facile romanticism caused by a moonstricken
craving for public power: "they [men] are so obsessed by public affairs that they see the world as by moonlight, which
shows the outlines of every object but not the details indica-
tive of their nature." Nor does the female principle escape
criticism. If men are awed by group values, women ignore
them. This indifference to trade and statecraft stales the female principle. By neglecting values outside their homes,
women fail to refresh their basic notions in the light of new
developments. Rebecca West again dips into etymology for
a label and extracts "idiot": "the word 'idiot' comes from a
Greek root meaning private person. Idiocy is the female defect: intent on their private lives, women follow their fate
through a darkness deep as that caused by malformed cells
in the brain." [14]

For a while, Rebecca West used the idea of sexual ambivalence to combine the best of the male and female strains. By
nourishing our sexual ambivalence, we can humanize public
enterprise and also infuse female tenderness with an analytical thrust. Rebecca West suggests a "mystical confusion of
substances" between men and women in *Harriet Hume*
(1929), and she praises Charlotte Brontë's power to speak
of "what is man in woman." [15] Beyond this passing theoretical interest, though, she does little to bring together the vir-

gin and the dynamo. In two of her short stories, "Life Sentence" (1930) and "The Abiding Vision" (1935), her leading male characters invite their female traits. Corrie Dickson and Sam Hartley (French *coeur*-heart) each blunder into gentle-heartedness after suffering financial ruin. This dualism is not reversible. One exercise seems to have convinced Rebecca West that women cannot entertain their male traits without surpassing men in lunacy. Corrie Dickson's wife Josie (or the more practical "Josephine" during office hours) is the only woman who foresakes family for business. At any rate, the idea passes out of currency in Rebecca West's work after about 1935. Since then, she only ascribes womanly qualities to men, as in the cases of Napoleon in *Black Lamb and Grey Falcon* and Göring in *A Train of Powder* (1955), for satirical purposes. The technique does not signal an enlargement of moral vision. It focuses angrily on individuals she disapproves of and degrades them by explaining their public acts as corollaries of sexual depravity. Dogmatic and judicious, Rebecca West is not above neglecting forensic niceties when fired.

Other murmurings of her feminist bias occur intermittently in her nonfiction. The arch-foe of love, sweetness, and reason in recent history is Napoleon. Napoleon can do nothing right. His itch for conquest and his ignorance of the arts of peace created imbalances that still perturb Europe. He also helped inaugurate "the masculinist and capitalist world" [16] that reached from the early nineteenth century to 1914. When western imperialism collapsed, first because of the rise of Prussian militarism and next because the Orient and the United States learned to provide for their own material needs, it had no human reserves to draw upon. The 1914–18 war was historically inevitable.

The age of Victoria had its spokesman in a complex man who was torn from his parents and again torn from his national culture while still a boy. Kipling ranged with bravado over the mannish landscape of the Industrial Revolution: long before bolshevism, he saw the excitement and romance of machine production. His passion for duty, efficiency, and machinery made him "the presiding genius of his time." [17]

Now that material expediency has gone out of fashion, it has become a matter of social conscience to question mechanical modes. Rebecca West contributes to this inquiry by recommending that we leave our machines and learn to enjoy the fruits of mechanized industry. Relaxation is something to be learned. The process of withdrawal and then settling into oneself entails, primarily, the maturity of self-acceptance. Rebecca West complained in *Ending in Earnest* (1931), a log of literary essays written for *The Bookman* in 1929–30, that English literature discourages adult attitudes. Modern British drama is weakened by an "obsession with immaturity" and a "clinging to youth." The most recent expression of this "cult of infantilism" [18] was provoked by the 1914–18 war: because grown-up men had to fight and risk their lives against the Germans, it was safer to remain a boy. The insistence in the early work of Christopher Isherwood (b. 1904) and Anthony Powell (b. 1905) upon the guilt of a generation of young Englishmen who did not see combat turns Rebecca West's feminism full circle from an alleged mania to prophecy.

Infantilism not only breeds social disorder. It also undermines the soil in which social relationships grow. Only maturity can generate the healthy interchange between an organism and its surroundings that Rebecca West calls process. Process is her most encompassing doctrine. Reconciling her dualism, it captures the best aspects of the male and female principles. Like love, it promotes happiness, freedom, and fullness of expression. But unlike love, which bursts forth like divine grace, process is slow, steady work. It may be defined as the sum of man's civilized energies, or, perhaps more accurately, as the application of civilized energies for civilizing purposes. Accumulative in character, it draws its strength from two main sources: a close acquaintance with many things over a long time and an openness to new experience. Each nature obeys a different process. Process, in turn, shapes identity out of the raw stuff of nature. It works through a self-generating rhythm, or ecology, that cannot be rushed. Her dislike of chance, disorder, and violence makes slowness a virtue in Rebecca West: cream does not pour quickly. This conservatism applies generally. An overnight public success in *The Fountain Overflows* (1956) damages everyone concerned with it, despite its glamor and high color. Analogously, we read in *The Thinking Reed*, "There was a definite process by which one made people into friends, and it involved talking to them and listening to them for hours at a time." [19] As processes, architecture, literature, and politics must foster the same fluid interchange. A building is obliged to comment on the activities conducted both within it and around it. Thus the Chartres Cathedral says something about the French experience of religion. It is fitting that one of Rebecca West's favorite writers, Thomas Hardy, is an architect endowed with the architect's power of committing himself to the materials of his art. Hardy is neither doctrinaire nor intellectual; his wisdom is much earthier. A craftsman, he learned from the roughness and toughness of the substances he worked with. His greatness as a writer is the ripe yield of his rootedness in British life.[20] Henry James enjoyed no such intimacy with natural resources or craftsmanly techniques. His exile is reflected by his shallowness. The rootless James is "incapable of forming a philosophy." His artistic aloofness bypasses the vibrations sounded by cultural movements. To use a familiar contrast in Rebecca West, he does not know what makes an event an experience. He fails to appreciate Rome as the externalization of man's civilizing impulses, i.e., the mastery of reason and love over environment.

> He failed to envision the Roman Empire save as a source of agreeable ruins which, since he did not understand the spirit that built them, he imagined might have been made still more agreeable. Their vastness did not impress him as the merging-point of the geological record and history, but stirred in him that benevolence which is often aroused by clumsy largeness. He patted the Roman Theatre at Arles as though it were Jumbo at the Zoo.[21]

Process underlies Rebecca West's admiration for Mestrovich, the fourth-century Slavic bishop who gained for his communicants the right to say the liturgy in their own language. The meshing of styles, natural resources, and institutions within a culture creates the solid dignity that is the best feature of nationalism. Rebecca West admires nationalism's desire to hammer selfhood out of the indwelling process of tradition. Nationalism, at best, is the collective effort of a people to achieve an organic independent character.

Nationalism merits praise for the same reason that imperialism invites scorn. Imperial expansion violates the process of government. A major argument both in *The Court and the Castle* and *The New Meaning of Treason* (1964) is the contractual basis of government. Without reciprocal obligations, there can be no civilized arrangements between people; a ruler may only demand loyalty from his subjects in exchange for protection. The buccaneering imperial spirit rarely invokes this contractual principle. To exploit cheap labor and raw materials, an agency will set up a military dictatorship, which, ruling by fiat rather than consent, severs the invaded country from its vital organs. Controls derive arbitrarily and unlovingly from without rather than growing naturally from within: process is murdered. Imperialism and process, in fact, are incompatible. Before a colony can yield a profit, the colonizing power must confiscate all money and property belonging to the natives. This can only be done by force. The practice defeats itself because no government can ground itself in military strength; power will simply pass from the old to the young and from usurper to usurper. The Roman and Napoleonic conquests prove that seizing a country and governing it are two distinct operations. The dangerous tendency to develop military strength at the expense of administrative skill is pointed out many times—not only in recent literature, but also in the dreams of foreign conquest entertained by the Axis powers in World War II.

Colonialism degrades all. It is no surprise that Clara and Piers Aubrey in *The Fountain Overflows* both have brothers who died in India at a young age. Imperialism's moral indifference to conquered territories destroys creative interchange. The moral level of imperialism never rises above opportunism. Ironically, his ignorance of the conquered territory makes the imperialist a bad profiteer. His life has lost meaning because of his ignorance of slow, civilized procedure. He is adrift: he fails to keep up with his own developing national tradition, and he rakes the national tradition of his victims. His only refuge is in a sentimental jingoism.

Life cannot travel too far from its source, and it blights the life that is native to those parts. Therefore it imprisons all its subjects in a stale conservatism, in a seedy gentility that celebrates past achievements over and over again.[22]

Process has another natural enemy in gambling. To surrender choice to chance is as easy as subduing it to commercial self-interest. Both operations—chance and financial greed —dazzle with surface glamor: both offer adventure: both reject reason and love. But while spheres of influence reduce all to material profit, gambling adds a hideous refinement. It reduces all to nothing. Gambling is despair because it rejects out of hand the few aids culture has marshalled to fight off inertia. In short, it exaggerates the natural advantages the universe has over us. The casino in *The Thinking Reed* has no windows or clocks: gambling attacks all civilized values, including space and time. This wilderness of numbers is an apt setting for tragedy. Empty, abstract, and void of human themes, numbers seal life inside a moral vacuum.

The only people who can endure gambling are those who have a special neurosis on the subject . . . or people who have said "No" to the Universe, who do not want to find out about things. If one has said "Yes" . . . time spent in a casino is time given to death, a foretaste of the hour when one's flesh will be diverted to the purposes of the worm and not of the will.[23]

Is this disgust for gambling disproportionate? neurotically obsessive? The answer to both questions must be negative. Gambling excites the death instinct; neither artificial nor unnatural, it is a corollary of our divided nature and must be reckoned with as such. A force that spoke less directly and less clearly would not be a menace: "Everything that happened in this room . . . appealed to something fundamental in human nature. The place had its power." [24] This power persists. Harry Sherman, the British bookmaker whose trial Rebecca West reported for *Harper's* in 1949, rouses both her respect and her fury. His charm, good sense, and conservative personal habits chime pleasingly with an artistry that Sherman indisputably brings to his profession. Yet his gifts are not humanized; abstractions, they can neither be shaped nor shared. Sherman's neglect of culture twists his art into sorcery.

Her hostility to gambling does not rob Rebecca West's thought of freshness and wonder. She is not trying to squeeze life into a system of moral imperatives. Her conservatism stands close to that of Joseph Conrad. Both writers urge collective action to harness the irrational. But whereas in Conrad unreason runs to anarchy, in Rebecca West it first runs to bigness. When things get big, they become hard to manage or control. Size dictates Harriet Hume's preference of chamber music to symphonies. Harriet argues that bigness leaks into diffuseness and disunity; the instruments in orchestral works carry too small a part of the composition to claim any vital function. For the musical crumbs thrown by the composer to the musicians do not feed the musicians' artistic imaginations. Rebecca West also says in *The Thinking Reed*: "The cast of a legitimate play . . . hardly ever exceeds a moderate number, since a theme cannot be crisply expounded by too many mouths." Its mass of "insufficiently related objects" makes Joyce's *Ulysses* "logically unsound." [25] There is a tight consistency between Rebecca West's artistic practices and her critical preachments. For, although her novels sometimes misfire, their stripped economy of character, setting, and plot cannot be faulted.

Dispersion infects political and social history just as it does art. Paris, "the best of all cities," [26] has resisted bigness by remaining a village in spirit. Anchored in a tradition not commercial, Paris keeps the sturdy compactness of preimperialist Rome. The wit and elegance usually associated with the city stems from an inherited allegiance to reason. Paris did not gain eminence by trial and error but by bending her energies to the service of the mind. Here is process at its finest—natural, self-renewing, and mindful of its bounds.

Paris's opposite, until 1945 anyway, is Vienna, seat of the Habsburg dynasty. Viennese art and Viennese political history share an ignorance of simplicity and economy. Starting in the nineteenth century, the Austro-Hungarian succession grew progressively unable to meet its material needs. Through greed and stupidity, the Habsburgs opened an economic rift between Vienna and the rest of the Empire. Instead of healing the rift internally, the Habsburgs looked for solutions abroad. Here lies the source of much of the political distress of our time. Big nations do not respect small ones —even when the small ones have achieved a higher civilized standard. By attacking Serbia, Austria-Hungary first violated Serbian independence and then, owing to cultural differences, forced an unworkable federation of Balkan duchies and principalities.

The Industrial Revolution began this suicidal trend—the concentration of wealth and power in cities. Vast, intricate towns in England and the United States lost the vitality of country life. The urban industrial worker, in particular, lost touch with natural process after being lured from the countryside. Imprisoned by automation, he had no materials or techniques with which to learn a craft. Moreover, since the urban gentry sneer at weaving, farming, and baking, the machine hand was actively discouraged from acquiring skills.

The social breach within capitalist economy has been widened by a tendency of management to keep too much of the profit and all of the executive controls. The supreme lesson of recent history is the perversity of our basic values. The historical practice of removing men from their farms and then denying them any access to dignity has produced a type —the dispossessed urban proletariat. He buys his groceries prepackaged without knowing any of the steps by which they reached him, and he turns a switch or presses a button when he wants to be entertained. In politics, he shirks the contractual arrangements imposed by government. His is a slavery of impotence, not one of oppression. Never having enjoyed the process of bringing things to life, he oversimplifies life. Never having been taught reason, he satisfies his needs by stealing and murdering. He first materialized as Luigi Luccheni, the assassin of Queen Elizabeth of Austro-Hungary in 1898:

He belonged to an urban population for which the existing forms of government made no provision, which wandered often workless and always traditionless, without power to control its destiny. It was indeed most appropriate that he should register his discontent by killing Elizabeth, for Vienna is the archetype of the great city which breeds such a population. . . . He made no suggestions, but cannot be blamed for it. It was the essence of his case against society that it had left him unfit to offer suggestions.[27]

Luccheni has amassed both muscle and manpower. He appears now as Pinkie Brown in Graham Greene's *Brighton Rock* and as Frederick Clegg in John Fowles's *The Collector*. In politics he is called Mussolini or Hitler. Once he gains power, his single-mindedness makes him hard to unseat. For a one-party state must quell free inquiry. It can never afford the risk of admitting evidence that may weaken the official public creed. To secure the loyalty of its followers, the state must promote the fiction that it has attained the zenith of civilization. Political opposition is thereby viewed as an insane attack upon science and justice and is treated as such — by a cadre of jack-booted militia.

Rebecca West knows that any dictator, having purged his state's political machinery of checks and balances, can work more efficiently than the head of a democratic government. A major operational handicap of democracy is the priority it gives to size: "The vastness of the Labor party is a source of weakness as well as strength." [28] (The specific indictment, incidentally, is merely a matter of timing. When the sentence was written [1949], the Tories were not in office.) No political party can rise above the apathy and opportunism of its members. Sophisticated espionage techniques, furthermore, owing to democracy's inherent commitment to free interchange, cause much more hardship in an open society than in a closed one.

Conceding that a dictatorship is nearly unshakable once it asserts itself, Rebecca West concludes that civilized man had better prevent the occurrence of a chain of incidents that will call for totalitarian devices. One preventative measure is the restoration of process through increased social fluidity, i.e., a less doctrinaire and more participatory democracy. Another is art. Art deals with fundamental questions of being and thus transcends violence, espionage, and that new corrosion, "internationalism"—a form of souvenir art usually found in booths and counters of large train stations. The art form with which Rebecca West is most familiar is literature. Unfortunately, she has no coherent method to support her claim that art can reform society. Yet she has probably gone as far as anybody toward externalizing art as a network of social principles. In 1929 she stepped within the dovecote of romantic criticism, ranging herself alongside DeQuincey, Pater, and George Moore. Like these men and unlike the more technical and analytical T. S. Eliot, she enjoins criticism to aspire to a "lyrical" description of the critic's personality. In 1932, her attack on Eliot's concept of tradition sharpened; again, she defined herself within the cult of personality. The authority of tradition was an "impressive ritual," "an organized pretentiousness," [29] that paralyzes thought: The creative spirit, she insisted, conflicts with, rather than reflects, inherited values. In recent years, though, Rebecca West has grown friendlier to tradition and less attentive to the imaginative powers of the critic: the creative spirit now belongs to the artist, and it leagues with tradition instead of opposing it.

Although no smooth uniformity is found in her work, it is both possible and profitable to trace Rebecca West's concept of art as a synthetic process. We shall begin with the artist, showing what he is and where he stands relative to other people—both artists and nonartists. We shall then assess the status of art in relation to other humanizing endeavors. This step is requisite to our next task, that of showing how the humanizing impulse energizes everyday life. Process both unifies and controls the dancelike metaphysic. At each stage, art obeys a logic that validates its growing range of application.

Rebecca West's aesthetic has the same tang as her social and political creeds: it is opinionated, strongly argued, and profusely documented. Her view of the artist as a man who addresses other men and who differs from his audience only in degree, is patently Wordsworthian. The artist can never detach himself from his fellows. But within him also pulse the working principles of the world at large. He is the true realist, the master of reality, and his job is that of a mediator. Our basic similarity to him enables us to meet him on the high ground of artistic creation. The artist makes us take him at his footing; that we can take him at all proves our underlying sameness to him. Starting with the modern notion of the artist as demon, Rebecca West never makes us wish this sameness anything but general. Her ruling metaphor for the artist is the battlefield.[30] Artists are battlefields, not men and women. Brooding and torn by conflict, they are not merely obsessed, as Graham Greene believes, but tormented. The artist's "fantasy," or vision, emerges dripping with blood from the private conflict between his will to live and his will to die. This struggle does not create art by itself, however; it only creates the psychological climate where art takes place. For art is never the offspring of self-absorption. The artist who remains self-absorbed is blind to the reality outside himself. His work, unrefreshed by bracing contacts with the material world, stales. The metaphor for this second ingredient of art is the sky. Art is a wedding of battlefield and sky. One artist who struck the singing note between the two requirements is Jane Austen. Jane Austen's characters are so natural and real because her ruling fantasy corresponded exactly to British society at the time.

The interaction of battlefield and sky, i.e., the artistic process, cannot be forced. Rebecca West's view of the interplay of conscious and unconscious drives within the artist is stated in her 1916 book on Henry James:

> Unless a subject is congenial to the character of the artist the subconscious self will not wake up and reward the busy conscious mind by distributions of its hoarded riches in the form of the right word, the magic phrase, the clarifying incident.[31]

In 1928 she rebuked Galsworthy for choosing subjects beyond his emotional grasp, "subjects . . . not within the scope of his artistic self." [32] In 1932 the dualistic creed of battlefield and sky takes on a Wordsworthian-Keatsian coloring. One thinks of "wise passivity" and "diligent indolence" when Rebecca West advises the artist to stay away from subjects intellectually attractive but not emotionally felt. By nature, the artist is not an activist. He cannot rush artistic creation by asserting it into life. Charlotte Brontë fell into the twin traps of sentimentality and sensationalism because of stresses in her personal life: "They [these stresses] committed her to a habit of activism which was the very antithesis of the quietism demanded by the artist." [33]

The artist, although racked with conflict, is the freest of all men. His practice of working out problems imaginatively gives him more scope than the "actionist" or man of deeds, who translates problems into bodily acts. The politician is just as handicapped. He wears the shackles imposed by his contractual obligations. By contrast, the artist is nearly divine:

> The duty of an artist is inclusive; he has to be hospitable to all manifestations of life so that he can get the broadest understanding of it. The first duty of a politician is exclusion; he has to drive out from his mind all motives but the public interest and from his party all rogues.[34]

The final advantage of the artist is the one he holds over the scientist. For, although the artist uses scientific techniques, the exchange is not mutual. Rebecca West is not talking about naturalistic fiction when she praises the scientific thrust of literature. Naturalism has no analytical power; it copies reality without interpreting it.[35] A scientific novel that both interprets and discovers while avoiding redundancy is Benjamin Constant's *Adolphe*. *Adolphe* conducts a controlled experiment in human response that generates a sociological truth.[36] Constant makes science work for him as it has never worked for the scientist: art can convey the complex emotions of its data where science cannot. Emotions, in fact, interfere with science. The scientist must extrude emotion in the interest of lucid detachment. Conversely, empathy is the artist's great gift and he must glory in it in order to probe human conduct.

Among the many gracious compliments Rebecca West

pays Arnold Bennett is a recognition in Bennett of that unique faculty which lifts the artist above his fellows—the faculty of impersonation. Bennett was a brilliant impersonator. Again Rebecca West strikes a close parallel with Romantic criticism. For just as Keats saw the poet as the least poetic of God's creatures (Shakespeare naughting or "nothinging" himself in order to create Iago and Imogen), Rebecca West calls Bennett's genius the impersonator's gift for empathy. Empathy, a raging appetite for life combined with an ability to love that life, projects Bennett so warmly into his characters that he validates their every action. The motivation in *The Old Wives' Tale* is perfect.

The doctrine of impersonation also has a foothold in nineteenth-century psychology: the artist's empathizing faculty and his suffering are often coterminous. A writer first creates and then becomes his characters because he cannot take life as it is. As in Schopenhauer and Freud, he escapes into a fabricated world due to his unhappiness with the natural world. Bennett, self-defensive about his incurable stammer, affected "the perfect Londoner": "Arnold Bennett wanted to do everything and to be everything. That determined his personal life and his literary career." [37] Dickens, too, blocked out the self that suffered the horrors of the London blacking factory, substituting one desensitized to pain. Beethoven is the supreme example of impersonation-as-sublimation. He proves, moreover, that a great artist can be a wicked person. Although his viciousness killed all his friendships, his power of empathy held this destructiveness in check while he was composing.[38] The empathizing faculty —once again, the talent to become somebody else at a given moment—is universal. This universality allows everybody to participate in art. It also explains why art can change a society into a civilization. Impersonation yokes art to morality. We can analyze the plight of a character in a book much more clearly than one of our own. Impersonation does the work of placing us in the character's predicament; we adopt his standpoint, values, and needs. But while we share his context imaginatively, we do not share it materially. To Rebecca West, this amalgam of involvement and detachment connects art to morals.

Here is where she parts company with Romantic criticism. The force that powers art to the level of morals is learning. The artist, therefore, must be learned, even scholarly. Art must relate the truth of its subject to as many other truths as possible. Instead of rising from a spontaneous overflow, it is a diligent exercise in comparative learning. Unless the artist builds a capacity—through learning—for universal reference, his work stales. A "natural ineptitude for acquiring systematic knowledge" spoiled both Henry James's fiction and criticism. Likewise, T. S. Eliot ranks far behind Edmund Wilson as a critic because of his "restricted field of reference." Robert Sherriff draws Rebecca West's fire because of *his* scant knowledge: "His subject [in *Journey's End*] seems to be the only subject he knows. He seems to have no other body of knowledge concerning the universe which he can use as a basis of comparison." [39] Comparison and allusion, analogy and metaphor: these unifying techniques make for a creative mingling of processes into a single process. The mass and force gained by this accelerating fusion establishes art as central to life.

The ingredients, the energies, and the applications of art all firm up civilized tradition. Art contributes to a fund of knowledge that serves civilization. Intellectuals are gregarious: they share each other's tools and techniques and they pool their findings. Like science and philosophy, art is adaptive. All three disciplines gather and store facts about the universe. All three, by making their inventories public domain, tighten our grip on reality. The scientist chooses stimuli with the same intuition and insight that impels the artist. By discovering a link between animal reflex and environment, Pavlov's *Conditioned Reflexes* performs the excellent service of teaching us how to survive: "Fido and Rover are partaking of a mystery of which, further up on the table, Cézanne and Beethoven are participants also." [40] Here is G. E. Hutchinson's fine summary of art's working partnership with science in the building of a culture:

Art is a storehouse of integrated perceptions. . . . The growth of a tradition is, therefore, a kind of implicit exploration, analogous to the more explicit growth of science.

Both activities are in fact similar and both bear the same relationship to the behavior of groups of people that the conditioning of the cerebral cortex bears to individual human behavior.[41]

Art says things that cannot be said any other way. Whereas science uses real materials, art uses imaginative ones. It can discuss man's social relationships, as in Shakespeare, Fielding, and Trollope, or it can seize upon man before he is socialized, as in Joyce and Lawrence. As has been mentioned, it works with data, real or representative, that the artist shares with other men. The decisive factor is the sharability of art; though the artist does not leave life as he finds it, he gains his audience's participation by beginning with a set of common, sharable experiences

For any authentic work of art must start an argument between the artist and his audience. . . . A major work of art must change the aspect of reality, for it is an experience of the order which breaks up the present as we know it, transforming it into the past and giving us a new present.[42]

The double task of scrambling and then remaking reality provokes another aesthetic tenet: art should be innovative and exploratory. Velasquez, for instance, accepted the creeds of his society; his conforming mind was not restless enough to create exciting art. His paintings, safe and docile, "deal with the organization of the already known." [43] The artist sacrifices his prophetic power if he leaves life where he found it. His standards cannot be those of society. Rebecca West turns from Velasquez to El Greco because El Greco's bold vision extends human experience. Art is paradigmatic; it describes people acting out common human principles. The actors are embodiments and the events they enact are types of events.[44] Art assumes the flexibility and open-endedness of tradition. While based in a set of social facts, it tests these facts against a new reality. The artist, thus, strives beyond the given or received. He strives for a harsh clarity and a wholeness which, surpassing present arrangements, provoke strong cortical reactions in his audience. Art, then, is kinetic, not static, as Joyce insisted in A Portrait.

The mythical aspirations of art are explainable by the gregariousness of the intellectual. The intellectual's craving for knowledge and his adventurous spirit make the intellectual community a working network of minds. Because an artist cannot detach himself from his background, art expresses a national culture. It takes its materials from a tradition both fixed and changing. Theme, then, is epical and mythical: epical because channelled through the life of a people; mythical in its inference that certain events recur and thus merit our attention. "The common fund of ascertained reality" [45] differs in each country. As an expression of common experience, art limns a national culture. The artist must be both political and nationalist to perform this feat. His nationalism tracks a painful dialectic: matching the struggle within him and the corresponding struggle between him and his society is the one pitting his society against God. By treating God as the final synthesis of his nation's unrolling drama, the artist endows his countrymen with godlike gifts. (The outstanding example of art as political metaphysic is Dostoevski's *The Possessed*.) Rebecca West herself writes in order to understand and express first truths:

> As I grow older I find more and more as a matter of experience that there is a God. . . . I hope I am working a way to the truth through my writing, but I also know that I must orientate my writing towards God for it to have any value.[46]

Some of Rebecca West's best work is found in her nonfictional writings. Today she is regarded by some as the outstanding nonfiction writer in the language. Her achievement as a documentary writer is the strenuous product of a lifetime's career. Whereas she wrote no novels for twenty years, 1936–56, she has always maintained a strong steady flow of nonfiction. Nor, as has been suggested, can this performance be confined. Although no literary critic per se, she wrote the first systematic critical analyses of Henry James and James Joyce, and, in *The Court and The Castle*, related Shakespeare cogently to major European political movements. Accordingly, *Black Lamb and Grey Falcon* stands as the master-

piece of travel literature in our century, and the magazine
essays that comprise *A Train of Powder* and *The New Meaning of Treason* bring to court reporting a heft and a command it never had before. What is the reason for this massive,
progressive, many-sided achievement? Its magnitude rules out
a detailed, systematic reading. (G. E. Hutchinson lists over
seven hundred items through 1951 in his "preliminary" 1957
bibliography.) What is more, Rebecca West has no personal
idiom or manner. Her only journalistic trademark is a general working apparatus which includes an abiding respect for
process, a twitching, incisive mind, and a warm heart that
glows most brightly when surprised. The closest we can get to
a coherent method is to note a few contours and character-
istics.

She meets so well her own requirements for an artist that
one is tempted to read her nonfiction as a preparation for
her fiction. Widely traveled and widely read, she knows
several languages and discusses companionably a spectrum of
subjects, including architecture, divorce, and nuclear track-
ing devices. And although her towering spirit has scanned
museums, concert halls, and courtrooms, some of her best
material originates in casual talk with obscure townsfolk.
She uses her large store of information as a wedge, not a
cushion. Instead of adopting a knowing manner, she respects
her reader and addresses him with humanity. Her essays fall
outside the tradition of the familiar essay of Addison and
Goldsmith. They are too hotly argued and solidly buttressed
with facts to qualify as polite learning. Her texture is uneven,
her irony complex, her tone sonorous and soaring. Her outstanding gift as an essayist may well be an ability to uncover
a striking generality around which she organizes her far-
ranging observations. All of her nonfiction reveals her as a
conceptualist. Hers is a unifying mind. Although she often
uses historical techniques—her important 1929 essay, "Tradition in Criticism," surveys literary criticism from Aristotle to
Pater—she usually isolates a kernel of theory and then shows
that kernel or germ nourishing a body of endeavor.

Her literary essays, like those of Hazlitt and Ste. Beuve,
which she admires, often interpret a writer's work psycho-

dynamically—as an offshoot of his personality. Accordingly, she strings the immense panorama of *Black Lamb and Grey Falcon* around a few events in Balkan history; these events, in turn, become paradigms of western culture. One of her favorite rhetorical stratagems is that of tracing an encompassing general truth to a single instance. Worth repeating in this context is her deduction of western literature from St. Augustine. Her 1932 essay on Charlotte Brontë develops the enigma, "Charlotte Brontë was a supreme artist; and yet she was very nearly not an artist at all." She calls Emmeline Pankhurst, the suffragist (1933), "the embodiment of an idea"; snobbery she labels (1938), "the eternally comic attempt of humanity to solve an eternally tragic problem." [47] Each of these essays describes a person or social trend acting out a behavioral law. In *Black Lamb and Grey Falcon* a woman in a Skoplje church strikes Rebecca West as "the very essence of Macedonia . . . exactly what I had come to see," and a statue of a seventeenth-century archbishop declares itself as "typically Slav." [48] At this point, it must be stressed that Rebecca West ascribes to no facile racism. Although she asks art to express a national heritage, she is never invidious. No culture or race is intrinsically better than any other. If one culture outpaces another, race is never a factor. Genealogical purity does not mitigate her dislike of the Habsburgs, and the heterogeneity of the Balkan peninsula fascinates her so much that she devotes an 1180-page book to the subject. Even unity must obey civilized process, nor does process exclude diversity.

Within a construct, however, Rebecca West will seek the emblematic, the symbolic, or the paradigmatic event which explains a complex drama. Thus Trollope's literary interests square with those of his society:

> The social landscape of the nineteenth century did not lend itself to poetry, and Trollope was so much a part of that landscape it was inevitable that he should be a novelist, and that his novels should be extremely prosaic. [49]

Just as consistent is the treachery of William Joyce ("Lord Haw-Haw"). An undersized social outcast given to street-brawls finds a home in the British Union of Fascists, an organization committed to disorder and violence. But men are more than the sum of their actions. The practice of cutting men to the pattern of paradigms does not deny the uniqueness of persons or the sacredness of life. The tissues of Rebecca West's prose pulse with rich, renewable life. To decry her quest for encompassing truths is to decry the myth-making of Joyce and Eliot. Like these monumental writers, Rebecca West shuns cheap mystical certainties. By placing an event within the context of a larger event, she can apply the test of process. Her lively wit also lends balance and freshness to her polemic: one of the judges in a 1949 trial "looks like a fusion of Mr. Pickwick and a mastodon." [50] Witty details like this prevent our knowing what shape an essay will take or what material it will use. The combination of depth and waggishness makes her unpredictable. As with her rolling, allusive style, to which it is bound, the ironic detail reaps the solid gain of heightening reader interest. She both arrests and surprises the reader by giving him more than he bargained for. She studies her subjects from unexpected angles, she brings new evidence to bear, and she applies unfamiliar criteria. One paragraph of her 1938 essay, "Snobbery," telescopes Leviticus, Mendel, Dr. Johnson, and the then chairman of the St. Pancras Borough Council.[51] Her 1945–46 report of William Joyce's trial treats us to delightful pocket histories of passports, Nazi propaganda techniques, right-wing British politics in the 1930s, and parliamentary rulings on treason. These dovetailings of far-flung events enrich us. They suggest new likenesses and, at the same time, probe new depths. Here is Hutchinson on the subject of her comparative rhetorical method:

> What has happened is far more complicated than one had thought before, memories and theoretical constructs drawn from all over human experience may be needed to deal with it.[52]

Rebecca West interprets culture as a function of intellectual history. The first chapter of her biography of St. Augustine sketches movements in the Church from A.D. 200–400.

Included in the survey are Manicheism, Neoplatonism, Pelagianism, and Donatism. These heresies, discussed with zest and authority, create a climate of ideas in which Augustine is best understood. A titanic theorizer, Rebecca West is fascinated by the interpenetration of ideas. Ideas are dynamic. They sink shafts into man's laws, his politics, and his art. She might have been describing herself when she said of Augustine that his "most severely abstracted thought is damp with . . . sweat." [53] Her prose is strongly sensuous. The dynamism of ideas accounts for the wealth of sexual tropes in her work. The *TLS* reviewer of *Black Lamb and Grey Falcon* came closest to her mythical monism when he spoke of her "mystical interpretations of events" as a tangy brew composed of "her higher ideal of civilization and . . . delicate sense of color and smell." [54] Rebecca West says in this book, "Existence in itself, taken at its least miraculous, is a miracle." [55] Man's appetite for ideas and ideologies confirms that miracle. The two late masterpieces, *The Fountain Overflows* and *The Birds Fall Down* (1966), describe the energy with which ideas charge into the bloodstream. One of the great merits of these works is their insistence upon the physicality of nonphysical experience. Irresistible facts strike not only the mind and the heart, but also the bowels. Perhaps experience only matters when it dents the flesh. Rebecca West does not bemoan the nightmare of history; nor does she rationalize the life of the senses: "I like hats, I like rooms with walls the color of autumn leaves, I derive pleasure from the recognition of character. I like strawberries; the people whom I like I love." [56]

Tough and tenacious, she can never be called an escapist. Our world—the one of racial violence, spies, and nuclear weapons—is the subject of her prose. Our world is the one she knows and is committed to. Our world is the world she serves and loves.

2

The Groove

Rebecca West did not take to the writing of prose fiction with the same easy aptitude she displayed from the outset in her criticism and documentaries. She might have been talking about herself when she censured Emily Brontë for forcing artistic creation before she was artistically ready. The four novels Rebecca West published between 1918 and 1936 raise deep questions—not about artistry but about the basic stuff artistry is made of. These works are enigmas: given their brilliance, they have no right to be so bad. Their soaring verbal cadenzas, masterful time-shifts, and nearly magical evocations of place fall flat because they are not the work of a novelist. By keying her early fiction to a muzzy Jamesian register, Rebecca West proves that a literary style cannot be arbitrarily annexed to suit any literary subject. Her fine tonal effects are not only wasted; bearing only marginally upon their subject, they destroy balance and unity. These books constitute a litter of brilliant fragments.

What they need most is the yarn spinner's or raconteur's gift for fresh, crisp narration. The events they portray are too stylized to be natural, and Rebecca West never endows her characters with the vigor to take charge of these events and give them a life of their own. Manner replaces meat; she even forgets her characters at times to weave linguistic embroideries out of words like "cogitate," "integument," "dubiety," and "ambulation." These embroideries choke life, as in *The Thinking Reed*, when her cadenced maunderings change sex into a lesson in art criticism:

She would not be afraid of those embraces which had so often reminded her, as she lay submerged in their tossing darkness, of the backgrounds of Delacroix's vaster pictures, of crimson curtains hanging from huge marble pillars whose capitals were lost in rich opacity, of stacked lances and jewelled and hieratic helmets, of immense fruits and iridescent serpents.[1]

These novels create a solid, globular world. Their warm, golden curves integrate well with their moral seriousness, and their well-knit interior logic offers civilized, intellectual pleasure. But their violation of probability and neglect of incident make them literary exercises rather than novels. Although novelistically designed, they are only imitations of novels.

The early short stories, including the four collected in *The Harsh Voice* (1935), can be readily summarized and dismissed. What disbars them from serious discussion is their artistic badness. Their preoccupation with American manners smacks both of the academic and the documentary. Swinging from the bracing provincial West to the stagnant East, they generate a clumsy, thesis-ridden satire. Rebecca West's ineptitude with the short story form is also seen in her endings, which are usually managed by means of a psychological principle, an item of previously withheld information, or an act of Jamesian renunciation. The heavy-handedness is most embarrassing when Rebecca West tries to reproduce an American speech idiom: "I ain't so old, really. Look at me—it don't hurt the eyes. It's only that I'm out of fashion." [2]

Technique and topicality in Rebecca West's first novel, *The Return of the Soldier* (1918), stand more securely. Visiting the recent past, she follows her master, Henry James, in keeping her story line simple in order to be complex elsewhere. The book's unified tone is also Jamesian: rather than cutting a sequence of events to the pattern of narrative, she tries to create a single sustained impression—the "felt life" that James called the novelist's main business. Set in 1916 and centered around a large country estate, *The Return of the Soldier* is a war novel with feminist overtones. It captures

the debunking mood of the period: severely critical in outlook, it uses recent intellectual developments to score both
social institutions and social creeds. Under heavy attack is the
concept of rational, individualistic man, Henley's Homo
Invictus. And, in the spirit of Lytton Strachey, Rebecca
West explodes conventions like the purity of the wronged
wife, the moral solvency of the British gentry, and the anti-
German hysteria that swept England during the 1914–18
war. What is fresh and new in this war novel is its viewpoint:
rather than going to battle, the author shows us what war
means to a woman who awaits the homecoming of a front-
line soldier.

The first chapter is striking. Thick, frumpish Margaret
Grey materializes in stately Baldry Hall to report that Chris
Baldry, the estate's master, has been hurt in combat. Suspect-
ing that Margaret may be practicing a heartless fraud,
Chris's wife Kitty shrinks in disgust from "her deplorable
umbrella, her unpardonable raincoat," and her "amazing
impertinence of the use of his [Chris's] name." [3] Before the
chapter ends, the women change positions. Margaret, it turns
out, has come to Baldry Hall in order to give, not to get, and
Kitty retaliates with ill-bred selfishness. Margaret has received
a telegram and a love letter from Chris, her sweetheart of
fifteen years before, now suffering from amnesia due to shell-
shock. Her tender concern for his family reveals her, not
Kitty, as fine and noble. By chapter 2 Kitty is already "a little
shrunk thing." [4] Earlier, she had prayed with Jenny, Chris's
sister and the narrator of the book, for their soldier's return.
Ironically, when Chris does come home, in the person of his
beloved, the wished-for miracle is refused.

Writing in 1934, Frank Swinnerton praised Rebecca
West's portrayal of Chris on the grounds that the amnesia
caused by shell-shock had never before served as a subject in
British fiction.[5] His amnesia makes Chris the sanest person
in the book. Its selective nature protects him against the
narrowness of his peers. It is not a breakdown but a refinement and a heightening. He has extracted what is precious
from the wreckage of time and works to preserve it. Although
red and rough-handed, Margaret materializes to him as

changeless beauty. His love confers upon both of them a timeless self:

> They stood with clasped hands looking at one another. They looked straight, they looked delightedly. . . . I reflected . . . how entirely right Chris had been in his assertion that to lovers innumerable things do not matter.[6]

Unfortunately, this rapture is snuffed out. Because Kitty and her clan can not afford to be judged by love's infinite requirement, love must be put to death. (Another stroke of narrative economy compresses the divine and the socially destructive character of love in a child's prayer, which goes, "Jesus, tender leopard," instead of "Jesus, tender shepherd.") Love runs counter to the public interest. So long as Chris loves Margaret, he is deemed unfit to return to his regiment. Being cured means loss and danger. At the end, when he is cut to the size of his empty marriage, his country's empty war, and his earlier, empty self, he reinstates himself as one of England's leading citizens. The title of the book takes on new meaning in the light of his resocialization. Margaret's triumph is that she unconsciously makes Chris thrive. Her tragedy is that modern society has no place for his authenticity. A first novel and a short one at that (185 pages), *The Return of the Soldier* shimmers with sensitively perceived and nicely handworked material. As has been suggested, it deserves to be a better book. The self-conscious style, though, keeps the story from telling itself. Here is an extract from a letter by Frank Baldry which explains that Chris is recovering from a brain concussion in a French hospital. The passage shows that Frank was in no hurry either to see Chris or to impart the news of Chris's condition to his immediate family:

> After having breakfasted in the town,—how superior French cooking is! I would have looked in vain for such coffee, such an omelet, in my own parish,—I went off to look for the hospital. . . . I do feel that the church has lost its grip on the masses.[7]

As Frank is an Anglican minister, Rebecca West may be using his obtuseness to discredit another social institution—

the English Church. If this is her aim, she must be faulted
for placing too much of a narrative burden upon too little
material. If her aim is different, she lays herself open to a
more serious charge, for Frank never reappears in the book.
Another serious error occurs when Chris describes exhaus-
tively the details of an afternoon spent with Margaret fifteen
years before: aside from neglecting the mind's limited powers of retention, the long summary violates the probability
that, deeply stirred by Margaret, Chris would never have
summoned so many details to begin with.

Jenny, the narrator, interprets her brother's selective
amnesia with compassion and discretion. But she does little
else: she instigates no action and she is untouched by the
actions of others. Rebecca West's failure to rouse narrative
movement from her narrative center forces her to resolve her
book with a deus (or diabolus) ex machina and a slew of
textbook theorizing. One imbalance provokes another.
Matching the author's limp response to Jenny is her avid
response to the then-new psychosexual criticism of modern
life. Ironically, neither the novel nor the society it describes
has the energy to conclude its business independently. If the
novel is unknown today, it owes much of its obscurity to its
clumsy use of now-outdated analytical techniques. Joseph
Collins, writing in 1923, called it "a fictional exposition of
the Freudian wish"; Walter Allen echoed this verdict forty
years later in *The Modern Novel* when he said, "*The Return
of the Soldier* reads like a dramatization of a case-history." [8]

But Collins and Allen distort when they reduce this ambitious first novel to Freudian case-study. *The Return of the
Soldier* tries many things and sometimes succeeds. Worth
repeating is its ability to show characters living in and even
modifying a climate of ideas. But because Rebecca West's
grasp of fictional method is more academic than instinctive,
the book's technique and subject do not jell. Whereas the
early chapters abound with Jamesian arabesques, the last
chapters have so little technique that the plot must go elsewhere for its motive force. To blame the book's failure on an
active preference for textbook psychology is to miss the point.
A failure the book certainly is. But Rebecca West capped

her novelistic fragment with a textbook ending because her imagination failed to supply a just and shapely finale.

The Judge is another exercise in what Joseph Warren Beach, in *The Twentieth Century Novel*, called "the well-made novel," as against the Victorian novel of action and plot. But it is sustained much better than *The Return of the Soldier*. Collins came close to describing it when he spoke of its theme as "conveyed indirectly, surreptitiously, atmospherically rather than verbally." [9] What *The Judge* is, is more vivid than what it says or does. Instead of reporting information, it exudes it, sweeping the denotative properties of words into its connotative rhythms and then shaping these rhythms into a fixed narrative center.

Thematically, *The Judge* sets itself the difficult job of applying Jamesian aesthetics to the post-Jamesian world. Conveyed indirectly is Rebecca West's dissatisfaction with hospital practices, evangelism, and the ravaging of the Essex countryside by real-estate speculators. A much steadier presence, however, is psychology. The book's shifting point-of-view technique—often the writer will describe the same experience from different standpoints—subordinates event and tempo to psychic inwardness. The working principle of the novel, then, is the assumption that event, as a thing in itself, counts for less than the psychic ingredients that make up an event. Along with *The Return of the Soldier*, *The Judge* belongs to the world of Freud, Havelock Ellis's *Psychology of Sex*, and Wells's *Ann Veronica*. Its emphasis upon sexual suppression and the Oedipus complex has also invited apt comparisons to *Sons and Lovers*. Yet, by describing the various events in her novel as a single drama, Rebecca West unifies her psychological data. Theme and technique coincide much more neatly in *The Judge* than in *The Return of the Soldier*.

The person who carries most of the narrative weight during the first half of the novel is seventeen-year-old Ellen Melville. Rebecca West gently ridicules her liberal-humanist heroine for her intellectual intransigence. Ellen's need to humanize her suffragette-socialist-atheist creed does, indeed, provoke mild laughter, even when she is uncomfortable. Be-

cause she sees people as causes or abstractions, she is not prepared for the dark animallike maleness of Richard Yaverland.
Nor has her intellectual crankiness taught her much about
herself; no humanitarian reformer, she wants less to change
society than to rule it herself. Not womanly enough to see
that she has moved Yaverland sexually, she tries to win him
intellectually. The novel's shifting point-of-view technique
brings out the humor in her attempts to be a model of reason:

> Though she was the least vain person in the world she
> was the most egotistical.

> He thought it very probable that never before . . . had a
> beautiful girl dressed herself so unbecomingly.[10]

But the humor is not uniform. Ellen begins and ends the
novel in tears, and it is a hallmark of her moral progress that
her tears grow more bitter and profuse with the passage of
years. Her growing up emerges as a human event taking place
erratically and reluctantly over a span of time. Ellen stumbles
into maturity; occasionally she backslides, and just as often
she moves forward because she has nowhere else to go.
Rebecca West describes through her the steps by which a
girl becomes a woman.

Book One of *The Judge* takes place in Edinburgh, where
Ellen works as a legal secretary; Book Two centers around
the Essex home of Yaverland's mother, Marion. Although
Ellen finds England and Marion much more complex than
Scotland and her job, she rises to the challenge. Her acts
trace a curve traced elsewhere by other characters at other
levels. The plot moves from a life that is also a death—Ellen's
academic awareness of things—to a death whose deadliness
comes from a vigorous participation in life. The path goes
from north to south, from indoors to outdoors, from institu-
tionalized to personal relations, and from security to loss and
shame. Oscillating in phase with these rhythms, Ellen gains a
true understanding of the woman's lot. One lesson she learns
is that she and Marion have never been free and that they
can never be free. Their common womanly plight emerges as
forcefully from the static elements of the novel as from its
moving fields of force. Death is the condition of *The Judge*:

Book One ends with a natural death, and Book Two ends more starkly in several unnatural deaths. The unmoving center that causes this death-drift is male insensitivity. Man's failure to love as fully as woman decrees that the reward for female beauty and goodness must be death. The male characters in *The Judge* act out this unlovely decree with accelerating urgency as modern society grows more mechanized and urbanized. Ellen's ordeal will probably be worse than Marion's.

The main target of the book's satire is Richard Yaverland. Yaverland's penchant for travel, his obsession with sex, his stern self-criticism, his strong mother, and his hatred for a father he hideously comes to resemble—these traits make him a present-day St. Augustine. Except for surrounding social conditions, Yaverland and the St. Augustine of Rebecca West's biography are practically one. Haunted by self-doubt, neither man can forgive himself or his parents for being creatures of flesh. Our first impression of Yaverland, then, like Ellen's, must be corrected: he is not the virile buccaneer he seems. Having just returned to the British Isles after an absence of thirteen years, he materializes spectacularly in the law office where Ellen works. (The unannounced appearance or surprise meeting is a staple of Rebecca West's fiction.) His exotic southern aura and the wet gray northern day—Yaverland enters the office like an imperious sea god—overpower Ellen. Called "the ghost of a drowned man," he merges with other men, like Adonis, the Christ of the tarot deck, and Eliot's Phoenician sailor, whose sea death brings life to others. The note he strikes for Ellen is one of primordial necessity: He compels her; she must conduct her earthly passage through the renewability he transmits. The sexual nature of the process is stressed by another primordial symbol, the snake. Ellen notices that Yaverland's "bare hand . . . was patterned like a snake's belly." [11] She cannot conduct her earthly business without participating in sin. But whereas she yields to sex, Yaverland cannot follow suit. As has been stated, his particular crime cannot be expiated. Rooted in his being, it is so much a part of him that his only escape is suicide.

Yaverland is the bastard son of Sir Harry Yaverland of

Torque Hall, now dead, and his madness stems from his self-appointed task of trying to overcome his illegitimacy. His impossible mission rests on his typically male faith in purposive action. A series of foreign adventures, redolent of flaming sunsets and burning shipdecks, has ended in his becoming a chemist specializing in explosives—explosiveness representing action in its tightest, most compressed form. At thirty, he is a director of a firm that manufactures cordite, "the material of militarism, which is the curse of nations." [12] Heir to his father's scowling aristocratic pride, he wants to be one of earth's kings without first bothering to be one of its citizens. His frenzy of activity does not hide the fact that, by suppressing his origin, he has also suppressed both his mother and himself. Like Forster, Rebecca West believes that human problems do not dissolve in action, but in love and understanding. Evasive about the heart, Yaverland can know nothing of the holiness of the heart's affections. He is a perfect Bloomsbury version of a Meredith hero. His worship of science is simply self-evasive. Haggard and guilt-ridden, he ironically needs Ellen much more than she needs him:

> Love of this girl meant infinite joy and a relief such as nothing before had ever promised him from the black regiment of moods that had for long beleaguered him, self-hatred, doubt of the value of any work on this damned earth, a recurrent tendency to brood on his mother's wrongs until he was a little mad. [13]

What he forgets is that Ellen's love will embroil him in sex. As she will do in *The Fountain Overflows*, Rebecca West shows a man bringing about the calamity he most wants to avert. Yaverland is not sufficiently self-committed to commit himself to anyone else. Like his father, he must die young. For he becomes not only his father, but, more tragically, his father's crime. The failure is one of loving: "Always . . . it had been his chief care that nothing at all should happen to him emotionally." [14] Yaverland describes his author's conviction that love and happiness are only certifiable by process. And process needs, first of all, a securely seated self. He bemoans his mother's wrongs and then lets her face them alone for thirteen years. Forever fighting the fact that he is the product of a sexual act, he condemns both himself and Ellen to a moral death embedded in sex. So long as sex is something more than a toy or a weapon, he cannot face it. Rebecca West's portrayal of Yaverland's emotional deadlock is first-rate. Aside from pressing beyond received Freudian doctrine, it spells out, long before Auden's poems on T. E. Lawrence, the sexual cowardice of the dauntless captain and conqueror of men.

Marion's relationship with Harry Yaverland does not need detailed discussion. Harry is simply another sexual coward. Actuated more strongly by his public career than by loyalty to the woman he loves and their unborn child, he allowed his family to remove him from England during Marion's pregnancy. Marion then desperately marries her lover's butler, one Peacey, with the proviso that he will make no sexual demands in exchange for the protection he offers. Peacey, who is probably named for the Victorian murderer, Charles Peace, then rapes Marion and fathers the pale simpleton later called Roger.

Marion's efforts to love Roger have the reverse effect of making her more appreciative of the merits of her first son. At the end, she kills herself, surmising that only her death can free Richard for a healthy marriage with Ellen. Her final reward for doing the loving work of two parents is the singular madness of judging, sentencing, and executing herself. Yet her suicide yields no gain. As soon as she dies, Yaverland kills his witless half brother, his reminder of the stench and filth of human flesh. The act is empty: Rebecca West's men seem to prefer any drastic action over the prosy business of settling down with a family. By contracting out of adult responsibility, Yaverland adds his sorry share to the novel's theme: that, unable to muster the outgoings of love, men heap misfortune upon women. Ellen has agreed to become Yaverland's mistress before he turns himself over to the police. Although he will probably be put to death, others will pay more dearly for his crime. The unwed mother and the murderer's bastard child will suffer long after Yaverland's fatuous romantic destiny has run its wasteful course.

The structure of *The Judge* does not split into two breach-

less halves. It has already been suggested that Ellen's innocent love of Book One and Marion's matronly sacrifice of
Book Two blend as a coherent experience. Rebecca West
smoothes the transition further by recounting Marion's
affair with Harry as a flashback in Book Two. Nor are Harry
and Richard Yaverland the only father and son in the novel
who, because of their weakness, devastate women. Mactavish
James, Ellen's seventy-year-old employer in Edinburgh, having married prosperously but not passionately, sees in Ellen
the repressed longings of his youth. But the wistful, fatherly
love he offers is too remote to help Ellen. In contrast, his
undersized son, Philip, resents being stung by her sexual
charms. Like his father, he will take the easy road of sacrificing love to prudence. In addition to meriting praise for unifying her theme, Rebecca West also deserves credit for her
striking phraseology. The following simile reverses the usual
movement from abstraction to concreteness; its sour, jarring
effect anticipates the similes of Graham Greene: "The strong
light fell on them like a criticism." [15] On other occasions,
concrete details serve a different purpose. Rebecca West's
study of the black clammy Edinburgh hospital where Ellen's
mother dies displays a Dickensian knack for combining
specific data. The squalor is unstinting down to the unfeeling
language of the hospital workers: "Everything possible is
done in the way of consideration for the feelings of friends
and relations!" [16] Another Victorian influence is Emily
Brontë. Like *Wuthering Heights, The Judge* shoots sparks
of white-hot emotion; its characters feel deeply and react
violently to each other. Yet, this abundance of intimate
heart-knowledge cannot be reduced to literary borrowing.
Rebecca West treats the subject of sexual love with both
delicacy and power. The relationship of Ellen and Yaverland
happens spontaneously; nor can they control its progress.
The "secret diplomacy between their souls of which they
knew nothing" [17] overrides words and deeds. It simply seizes
the lovers and holds them in an iron grip.

Unfortunately, Rebecca West's commitment to her materials is not warm enough to bring her book to life. *The
Judge* contains splendid effects but no surprises. Its attitude

is too rigid; it never wavers from its basic assumption that all socially established practices and institutions are wicked. Can a rich man's success always be traced to an act of sexual cruelty? Must male sexual love always resolve itself into the three-tiered formula of passion, cowardice, and desertion? Is organized religion always ascertainable as a tambourine-shaking minstrel show? Roger Peacey obeys probability when he joins the ranting evangelist sect, the Hallelujah Army. But his reason for joining—that Jesus's love is so strong it overlooks human weakness—deserves more compassionate scrutiny than the thick brushstrokes of Rebecca West's satire allow. Even the epigraph of the novel—"Every mother is a judge who sentences the children for the sins of the father"—adds a cynical touch; for the novel is dedicated to the memory of Rebecca West's mother. It is only fair to mention, though, that the cynicism is sweetened by the fact that the writer's mother and the "bonny wee thing" [18] Mactavish James sacrificed to commercial expediency each have the same first name, Isabelle.

Other objections to *The Judge* may be easily marshaled. The foregoing rehearsal of the novel gives an impression of artistic solidity. The impression is false. For a five-hundred-page novel, *The Judge* is poor in drama. Although its theme strikes deeply, it often gets lost in long passages where nothing important happens. These passages make *The Judge* more anecdotal than dramatic. Again, Rebecca West permits herself stylistic or psychoanalytic flights at the cost of story. Descriptions like the following, in spite of their rich color, blur and encumber rather than reveal character:

> This [Yaverland] was the ghost of an Elizabethan seaman. She could see him, bearded and with gold rings in his ears and the lustrousness of fever in his eyes, captaining with oaths and the rattle of arms a boat rowed by naked Indians along a yellow waterway between green cliffs of foliage. Yes, she could not imagine him consulting any map that was not gay with painted figures and long scrolls.[19]

A worse distraction is caused by the novel's compositional mode. Braybrooke's complaint on the subject, registered in

1926, still holds good: "The solid blocks of very close print in which Miss West indulges are not only extremely irritating but tend to obscure the meaning." [20] *The Judge* does not have enough dialogue to brighten and balance its long narrative interludes. Its solid blocks of print are its most vivid feature. Clamped in the death-lock of the Jamesian manner, it is not a pleasant book to read. That Rebecca West did not try another novel for seven years suggests she may have felt some of this unpleasantness herself.

Harriet Hume: A London Fantasy treats the same concerns and reflects the same attitudes as the two earlier novels. But its fantastic technique is so remote from that of *The Return of the Soldier* and *The Judge* that it represents a new start rather than a development. In *The Court and the Castle*, Rebecca West speaks of *The Tempest* as a fantasy. A more extended comment on fantasy appears in a 1929 review, where she insists that, far from being escapism, fantasy has artistic responsibilities more rigorous than those of realistic fiction.[21] Unfortunately, the fantasy in *Harriet Hume* falls short of her critical requirements. Of all the early fictions, it is the most artificial and the most arbitrary. An academic exercise, it says nothing new about its subject and does nothing exciting with its materials.

The fantasy form creates outstanding liberties with natural laws and with laws of probability. Encompassing the Adam brothers, two notable eighteenth-century architects, Gladstone, and Dean W. R. Inge, a popular radio theologian of the 1920s, the time sequence of *Harriet Hume* surveys London's history alongside the friendship of Harriet and Arnold Condorex. Other characters have names like Mr. and Mrs. Badger-Gayme, Lord Scorchington, and Prince Camaralzaman, and there is an organization called the Union of Anglican Housewives Opposed to All Amorous Delights. The dreariest conglomerate in the book, however, is a sentence that extends to 224 words, refreshed by only three semicolons.[22] Rebecca West does not seem to have learned much from experimenting with fictional technique. Her London is barren, and her fantasizing does little to smooth the roughness between the story and the way the story is told. Again, she weakens dramatic impact by inserting several long set passages which neither advance the plot nor extend it.

Harriet, the title character, deserves a better book. For she is woman incarnate; Hutchinson calls her Rebecca West's "most ethereal character, her quintessential distillate," and "a white witch." [23] Her connection with David Hume suggests a skeptical rationalism, but one grounded in female tenderness and sympathy. The purling liquids and spirants of her name picture the lightness and grace that attend this new rational spirit. Harriet is reasonable enough to know the supremacy of human love. Her love for Arnold Condorex is so lucid that she can read his thoughts. This ability to join in the reality of another person is the fullest expression of love. Harriet is a healer; it is not by accident she stops at the statue of Jenner in Kensington Park. She is a priestess; her large home, its design, and its furnishings invite elaborate comparisons to churchly things. An artist, she is also socially unfixed or classless, as free and as imperishable as a spirit. Aside from leaguing her with Stephen Dedalus, Joyce's artist-outlaw, Harriet's weak eyes suggest an inner gleam that perceives truths beyond the range of normal sense experience. Throughout the book, her age, social rank, religion, and family background remain undefined. Like an idea or a principle, she just *is*; but again, like an idea or a principle the *is*, is everything.

All art strives for unity, and the most integrated art form, blending form and content, is music. Plato saw music as the groundwork of social justice, and Conrad called it the highest art form. One irresistible energy of music is its power to speak a universal language. Harriet's musicianship, by going beyond her music, partakes of some of this universality. She speaks of the similarity of music and politics: both disciplines promote greater organization: both help us cope with reality: both express a collective will to freedom. Yet Arnold snubs this musical ideal. He keeps calling himself Harriet's opposite, forgetting the ability of music to resolve opposites. His particular interest as a politician, he insists, is negotiation and the struggle for fame, not political theory. Just as Harriet stands for prime woman, he is the archetypal man, or lunatic—the public man who gauges his values by the values of other people. He is not self-determined or self-acting. He feels watched, insecure; he worries obsessively about his reputation. And because Harriet cannot add to his public image or help him gain public power, he relegates her to the lonely lot that, ironically, measures a woman's worth in Rebecca West: "It is the special hardship of women that it is their destiny to make gifts, and that the quality of their giving is decided by . . . those who do the taking."[24]

In denying Harriet, Arnold both denies and denatures himself. But she also needs him as badly as he needs her. Their opposition is only roughly one of spirit and matter. The rolling vowels and deep-sounding consonant-clusters of his name stir more pleasant associations than the name of his political rival, Rampound. Were Arnold a thoroughgoing self-seeker, he would not have noticed Harriet to begin with. Conversely, her association with snakes and gardens endows her with a sexual identity. She is, in fact, quite frank about her sexual availability and emphasizes the point by eating cherries. Another humanizing touch is supplied by her identification with the dove. The dove of peace is the natural enemy of society's prevailing arrangements. It cannot flourish amid materialism, self-deceit, and the lust to public power. Rebecca West's reading of the significance of the dove is stated sharply in her 1933 monograph, A Letter to a Grandfather:

> Supremely apt symbol of the spirit, the full life of which is lived only by certain human beings and by certain parts of human beings, which flies forth and pillages the material life with its sharp, greedy beak of criticism, while the natural man stands by and curses.[25]

Harriet's transcendence and her self-destructiveness, then, dwell inseparably in the same nerve cell. Her uniqueness is both a blessing and a curse, for she cannot secure her ends without risk. Her refusal to distort or weaken her requirement frightens Arnold away; yet this steadfastness also brings him back.

If Harriet remains pure and unchanged, Arnold grows

cumbrous and careworn. As his roars grow more thunderous, they also grow emptier. In the last chapter, he is out of joint with the world: he is more slave than master to his ten house-servants, and, although he owns three fine cars, he does not have the cash to buy a loaf of bread. This disjointedness is self-inflicted. Early in the book, he acknowledges that Harriet meets all his needs; it only remains for him to perform the reasonable acts of marrying and settling down happily with her: "You are as dear to me as if I had known you all my life, which I have not, and as exciting as if I had seen you for the first time this afternoon, which I have not either." As ideally matched as he is to Harriet, he does not propose marriage. His insecurity drives him, instead, to trade love for fame. In this respect, the psychologist who best explains him is Adler, not Freud. His lower-middle-class Jewish back-ground accounts for his bleats of masculine protest: "I shall not rest until all men have admitted that I am their peer; ay, and beg me to make admission of equality." [26] Logically enough, Arnold's plight is the plight of the self-made man. Surrounded by honors, titles, and riches, he has never culti-vated a soul. He backs away from love because he cannot handle anything not earned by hard work; his gift for com-promise and negotiation have not prepared him for the truth that love is always freely given, never earned. The moral of *Harriet Hume* is that people need other people. Accustomed to using people as ciphers in his political schemes, Arnold has no life apart from his public self. He dies within a few hours after his removal from public office. Having been caught embezzling government funds, he no longer has a title or a reputation to negotiate with. The last chapter of the book begins with him looking into the mirror: his world has gone so flat, stale, and tight that he is even closer to death than he realizes. The mirror is both his last refuge and the chief symbol of his public career. Lacking a fund of human reserve to draw upon, the bankrupt ends his life alone, in disgrace, and possibly as a suicide.

Turning from the last to the first chapter of *Harriet Hume* is both inviting and instructive. The book opens with Har-riet and Arnold running down the stairs from Harriet's room. If they have just been lovers, they grow progressively apart as the book continues: in the first paragraph they pause to kiss: Arnold takes his hand from her waist in the second paragraph; by the end of the chapter, the following day, he is about to take a government post in India. Each succeeding chapter treats a later meeting of the former lovers. The meetings occur at irregular intervals of from five to twenty years and usually at a different season. They prove that Arnold has never exorcised Harriet. After his mind cracks in the last chapter, he becomes driven to punish her. And united with her he is, but not in vengeance. (Joseph Warren Beach, on the other hand, holds the view that Arnold "shot her dead and then killed himself.") [27] His night journey through the London streets to her home signals a new dawn. He is first arrested by two policemen who discover him crouching near her window with a loaded pistol. But Harriet intercedes. The redemptory female who intercedes on behalf of the sinning male is mentioned several times in *The Court and the Castle*. The idea is never dramatized more vividly in Rebecca West's fiction than in *Harriet Hume*. The female who suspends secular justice in favor of mercy performs an act of grace. By welcoming Arnold into her home, Harriet both rescues and redeems him. And by accepting more than he deserves, he testifies personally to the ethic of forgiveness. The musical ideal has been achieved.

This singing conjunction of deed and principle, of male and female, and of Hebraic and Christian, occurs perforce after death. Even the prophetic Harriet does not know what the next day will bring. It is too bad that the narrative energies which bring about this resolution balance so badly. *Harriet Hume* is a stuffed, disjointed book. Untrimmed and unassimilated data of all kinds slow down the plot and blur the theme. Of all Rebecca West's longer fictions, it would lose the least by being rewritten as an essay. It is, in fact, a polemical essay in disguise. This criticism is another way of calling *Harriet Hume* her weakest book.

The Thinking Reed follows a familiar pattern: it juxtaposes a female character who stands for an orderly housekeeping grounded in sexual love against a male with lavish material advantages but little human warmth. But whereas the archetypal Westian male formerly used his money and power to hide an emotional void, he serves a more complex morality in *The Thinking Reed*. Rebecca West disperses her feminist grapeshot among four male characters, at least one of whom is morally superior to her heroine.

None of Rebecca West's women has enjoyed the advantages of Isabelle Tarry Sallafranque, and none has been treated so roughly. The rough treatment, however, represents no change in attitude or stance: Rebecca West's feminism is held as closely and expressed as strongly in *The Thinking Reed* as it ever was. The rubs given Isabelle indicate an enlargement of moral position, not a shift. Referring to the book in *Black Lamb and Grey Falcon*, Rebecca West said that she once wrote "a novel about rich people to find out why they seemed . . . as dangerous as wild boars and pythons." [28] The phrase, "to find out," captures the tentative, exploratory quality of *The Thinking Reed*. It is at once her most provisional and her most cheerful novel; the questions it asks outnumber the claims it makes. Isabelle says at one point that "nothing like what she was experiencing had ever been recorded." [29] Although she exaggerates, her remark conveys one of her author's aims: to impart freshly and vividly the sensation of femaleness, i.e., what it is like physically and psychically to be a woman. Isabelle functions as no bursting reservoir of female goodness, but as an inlet into female experience. The descriptive techniques used to portray her negate fixed judgments in favor of a surprisingly Lawrencean love dynamic: instead of being worse, men are simply different from woman; nor may the difference be bridged.

This revisionist ethic, bracing and unbookish as it is, fails to quicken much excitement. The best of the early novels, *The Thinking Reed* is also the most conspicuously flawed. First, it smacks of moral decadence. A writer committed to public responsibility, Rebecca West draws critical fire by writing a comedy of upperclass manners during a time of great public hardship. Writers like Greene and Auden, by inventing new idioms, created a heightened vision of the

1930s. No such originality or heightening obtains in *The Thinking Reed*. Neither socially relevant nor poetically apt, the book exudes a drawing-room perfume that blunts serious thought. Its liveried servants, stuffed, varnished interiors, and artificial gardens relegate the book to the same escapist category as Monopoly and the spectacular Hollywood musical comedies of the period.

Yet it is easy to see how *The Thinking Reed* has remained the most popular of Rebecca West's novels. Its Jamesian and Lawrencean strains fit together comfortably. Like Isabel Archer (*The Portrait of a Lady*) and Milly Theale (*The Wings of the Dove*), Isabelle Tarry qualifies for the title, heiress of all the ages. An American of aristocratic French lineage, she has both everything and nothing. At twenty-six, she is "beautiful . . . nearly exceedingly rich . . . tragically widowed." She has nobody with whom to share her lavish gifts. "An only child, early orphaned, and early widowed," she is a classic case of the Rebecca West heroine who suffers unjustly and unfairly. Isabelle, though, remains cool; her "competent, steely mind," [30] she is sure, can subdue any crisis. Herein lies her comic flaw: an unreasonable commitment to reason and order.

For an individual who prides herself on her rational powers, Isabelle conducts a singularly irrational private life. Shortly after she goes to France, sensibly enough, to ease the shock of her husband's death, she becomes one man's mistress, a second man's near-fiancée, and a third man's wife. And she marries her husband, not for love, but for spite. In *Henry James*, Rebecca West raked Isabel Archer for marrying for a reason other than "the consciousness of passion." [31] By bestowing the name and the moral offense of James's character upon her own exiled heroine, Rebecca West establishes a working context for her thinking reed. Isabelle is both luckier and more self-deluded than her namesake, though. Her brightening outlook at the end of the book springs from the irrationality she scorns. Ironically, whenever she acts in the name of reason, she foments unrest. Only after her second marriage—which turns out much better than she deserves—does she realize that her earlier, more spectacular marriage to the famous aviator, Roy Tarry, was made empty by Roy's juvenile passion for speed and his accompanying fear of roots. (Also hinted at is the possibility that the daredevil pilot was sterile.)

At the outset, Isabelle finds herself, to her horror, the sexual slave of the handsome, elegant André de Verviers. De Verviers's failing, curiously, is a lack of verve: he is everything he appears not to be: insincere, cheaply theatrical, and scheming. He compensates for his lack of passion by noisily drumming up discord: rather than seeking an even, civilized keel for his romance with Isabelle, he stages emotional outbursts and burning reconciliations. To escape this "heated sort of wrong," [32] Isabelle encourages the suit of her deceased husband's friend and former classmate at Princeton, Laurence Vernon. A Virginia gentleman who belongs in a tradition neither commercial nor agrarian, Vernon poses a dignified answer to the pressing question of Isabelle's national ties. Unfortunately, he offers little else. Isabelle admires him less for himself than for the happy contrast he poses to de Verviers. Both the polished, poised Vernon and his cypress-bordered estate, Mt. Iris, represent an extreme as deadening as de Verviers's wild theatricals.

Ironically, she would gladly have married Vernon were the choice not taken out of her hands. Convinced that she can only free herself from de Verviers by performing a spectacular public disavowal, she throws his gift bouquet of flowers into the mud and tramples them—all in the presence of his servant. By a farfetched coincidence, this event takes place the same day she expects Laurence Vernon to propose marriage. By an incredible coincidence, Vernon happens to be visiting a neighbor of de Verviers this same morning. By a matchless coincidence, Vernon has stationed himself at the window of his friend's apartment during Isabelle's exhibition. He sensibly uses the occasion to change his mind about marrying her, thus creating for Isabelle a monstrous reversal of fortune. Moved by reason to spurn de Verviers, she finds herself rationally offensive to another man; caught in her own trap, she cannot fail to see that Vernon's rejection of her mirrors her own rejection of de Verviers.

The reversal brings out her worst features. In order to save face with Vernon, she dissolves the incident by reporting that she has decided to marry her persistent, but unlikely admirer, Marc Sallafranque (who, by singular coincidence, is expected shortly at the restaurant). Her motive for marrying Marc suffices to damn her. But Isabelle may also be keelhauled for her particular choice of a mate. By agreeing to marry Marc, she demonstrates for the second time in one day that her sexual preferences are actuated by sharp contrast. Marc's great attraction, aside from his availability, is his oppositeness from the urbane, sophisticated presence vexing her at the moment. Only her prideful stupidity keeps her from seeing that her life has become a shambles in which she has thoughtlessly involved an innocent person. (Later, at the nadir of her marriage, she is faced with the same kind of choice and responds much more keenly.) Although she learns to love Marc and even comes to speak of her "amazing good fortune in marrying him," [33] she never appreciates how truly amazing her good fortune is.

For her choice of a husband could not have been better. Marc Sallafranque is both the most busy and the most attractive male in the Rebecca West canon. Although he is wealthy, his ownership of a thriving automobile concern keeps him out of the leisure class. His exclusion from upper-class society works to his advantage: Rebecca West's rootless aristocrats comprise a tight circle of hard-drinking athletes hemmed in by vows of "wealth, unchastity, and disobedience to all standards." [34] Like any other primitive, barbaric society, the smart international set is tightly conservative. Social status and freedom, in fact, operate inversely; the only titled character in the book is also the least free. That Marc's riches are earned, then, provides a creative outlet for his energy. And energy he has. Isabelle says of him, "he seemed made all of one thick, rubbery piece." [35] This elasticity accounts for his vitality and bounce. Composed of well-wearing, springy stuff, he usually wins his point by dint of his staying powers. The "refusal to accept defeat" is a Jewish trait that applies directly to him. "Comically violent" and a "human barrel," [36] he is the vulgar commercial success, the buffoon. Yet Jewishness is not his only trait; Rebecca West also speaks of "Marc's close black curls," "the pouted thickness of his lips," and "his broad, flattened nostrils." [37] These physical features, along with Marc's frequent mentions of jealousy, turn the mind to Othello. Like Othello, Marc is natural and good-natured in the best sense: he loves rain, he is neither artificial nor vain, and he has a heart so noble that he naturally believes the best of everybody. To her credit, his energy and good will carry the day with Isabelle. Their marriage is warmly portrayed; details like the following generate a tenderness and intimacy the reality of which happily defies literary criticism:

> He turned a kind eye on her, he held his fingers crooked against his trouser-braid as he did when he wanted to give her a sign that if she stood close beside him she could hold his hand without people noticing.[38]

Isabelle violates both this love and the process that created it by defining love too strictly. The climax of the novel occurs during her pregnancy, which she enjoys as a total bodily thriving, a bracing fact that yokes her healthfully and purposively to her life-giving function. She forfeits this creativity and a good deal more. The background of her crisis is this: because Marc used some of France's Reparations Fund to rebuild his family's business, the government, to avert civic disorder, forbade him to gamble in public. When Isabelle finds him at baccarat, his defenses lowered by several boring hours with the international set, she creates a violent scene. The upshot is her private loss and public disgrace. She outdoes the prototypical Jamesian heroine who, by demanding too much, gets nothing. Within the framework of the novel, she betrays her moral unreadiness. Within the framework of Rebecca West's developing body of thought, her act shows that the intercessory female can do her job too well: whereas Isabelle's desperate act restrains Marc from gambling, it costs her both her child and her reputation.

This hideous scene occurs, appropriately, in the baccarat room of the Riviera gambling casino, Le Toquet. The time of the year, Easter, emphasizes the corrupting power of gambling; it thwarts natural process. Marc as well as Isabelle neglects his deepest obligations when afflicted by the gambling fever, by placing her in a moral position from which there is no honorable release. The lighthouse standing in the middle of the town adds to the expanding deathlike metaphor. The baccarat room, "the core of the life of pleasure in a town built for pleasure," [39] has a dull, sullen atmosphere that whets a natural human inclination for incoherence and breakdown. The incoherence and breakdown continue stirring in Isabelle long after she recovers from her physical ordeal.

Nothing makes sense to her after her miscarriage. Her mind and body are out of joint, and even the simplest material objects fail to cohere: "The lens of the air was undimmed, nothing was merged by dampness, every object was . . . distinct." [40] She visits spas in France and Switzerland in search of continuity and wholeness, but when she returns to Paris and Marc her world is still in bits. Rebecca West conveys the unrelatedness of her life through narrative structure: while chapter 10 ends with her greeting Marc, the next chapter shows her, without transition, entertaining another man in her bedroom.

Periodically, she has been receiving kind advice and encouragement from her wise uncle in California, Honoré. At the end, she outgrows her need of him, having achieved her own dignity and honor. Her scrappy love affair convinces her that her life is ineluctably bound with Marc's and that, moreover, rejection of the terrierlike Marc equals a rejection of life itself. By ceasing to hanker after rational explanations, she acquires a new reverence for life. In short, she acquires faith. Her willingness to accept an imperfect reconciliation with Marc and a marriage with an uncertain future constitute an affirmation, not a concession. As soon as she acknowledges that the tensions in her marriage cannot be talked out, her world takes on new tones and depths. A systematically arranged love, she learns, is incapable of surprise or renewal. The frayed edges of her marriage teach her to suspend thought in favor of feeling. By opting for something she can neither define nor control, she expresses confidence, for the first time, in the ability of her marriage to create its own safeguards and freedoms.

This self-confident, ungrasping sort of love gives rise to the novel's main symbol—a chandelier comprised of four golden eaglets poised to fly in four different directions. The "stiff yet gracious bands" [41] that restrain the wild beauty and fierce energy of the eaglets stand for civilization. By themselves, the four eaglets do not serve reason and love; like the four elements, the four humors, and the four seasons, they suggest the brute natural order: the number, four, in fact, designates the material world in most western systems of numerology. These natural forces must be civilized. Now civilizing to Rebecca West is not the same as weakening or distorting. Rather than denying natural impulses and rhythms, she seeks to balance them in a true singing tension. Like the traditional wedding ring, the encircling band of gold on the chandelier shapes noncivilized forces to civilized purposes. Concluding that it is better to organize man's usable energies than to squander them, Rebecca West uses her symbol to define Isabelle's two marriages:

> The ray of light from the landing showed her nothing but the four eaglets . . . winging their way to the four quarters of the globe, but held back by stiff yet gracious bands. It was so in marriage, when one loved one's husband. Wild things that would have flown away and been lost in the violent airs above the edges of the earth were restrained within four walls, to be perpetual in their beauty. [42]

Unfortunately, this symbolic array is wasted. It ranges itself brilliantly and powerfully, but in arid territory. For Marc is the only well-accoutred character in the book. The satire on the rich international idlers fails because of its muddy focus. Overriding Rebecca West's keen analysis of high society is the absence of dramatic wit. Her satirical edge is blunted by her latinate diction; in one place she follows a sixty-seven-word sentence with one of sixty-one words: at another place she disparages a character with the term, "lapidary fatuity." [43] She does not surprise with the pithy, telling

phrase, the damning self-disclosure, or the conversational pat-
ter that both defines and belittles. Her rich vulgarians are
simply rude and boring. Moreover, by refusing to let them
do anything right, she reduces them to embodiments of human failings. Phrases like "it was not the kind of fault men
outgrew," "thoroughly characteristic of her type," and "an
Englishwoman of this sort" [44] replace shapely character portraits. And because the book lacks shapely, well-defined characters, it lacks life. Her uneasiness with character, besides
cornering her into typing people, throws her narrative structure out of balance. The exposition on several characters
clashes sharply with the role these characters play in the plot:
Rebecca West will supply elaborate background data on a
character only to drop him shortly thereafter. What she does
not do is endow her characters with the crude animal vigor
to advance matters by themselves.

Unable to develop her plot with the aid of characters, she
assumes a knowing stance. A good deal of *The Thinking
Reed* consists of impressionistic evocations of places, trends,
and traits. The Rue de l'Universite, in Paris, for instance, is
rendered as "that long alley street full of amber antiquity
and little shops which have stewed in their stuffiness for centuries, so that it seems kitchen-warm on the coldest day." [45]
Although most of these descriptions have the uncanny right-
ness of tone poems, they rub the grain of the plot. By making
them do the dramatic work normally assigned to characters,
Rebecca West violates dramatic probability. Isabelle's bel-
letristic impressions of rural France and Switzerland are simply not the thoughts of a woman suffering from torn nerves
and sleepless nights. One must conclude that even Isabelle is
poorly drawn. Although Rebecca West knows her well
enough to use her as the novel's recording intelligence, she
cannot resolve her plot through Isabelle. Smuggled into the
last two chapters are a long unseated monologue, a new character, two letters, a cat, and two dogs. (In Rebecca West's
fiction, men run to dogginess, whereas women incline to
cats.)

Like its predecessors, *The Thinking Reed* attempts narrative sophistication but overlooks narrative fundamentals. Its

urbane characters and marbled, candenced language aspire toward a poetic ideal. But her master, who did bring to prose fiction a new poetic unity, would have disparaged her cultural rummages as "a saturation" and "an unseated mass" because they do not blend with the book's dramatic economy. The rich autumnal tones of *The Thinking Reed* are death-dealing. But whereas the book's stylistic evenness denies life, the rough edges and unglossed planes of her next book, *Black Lamb and Grey Falcon*, throb with vitality. The difference is primarily one of literary form. Rather than renovating her basic method, Rebecca West orchestrates the anecdotal elements of *The Thinking Reed* into the soaring disquisitions and speculations of *Black Lamb and Grey Falcon* and, in the process, almost invents a new literary form. When she returns to novel-writing twenty years later, she will be armed with a technique that clinches style and subject and shapes her material to the pattern of fiction without any loss in imaginative power.

3

The Court

The Court and the Castle is a gathering of talks Rebecca West gave while Terry Lecturer at Yale University in 1957. None of her other books relates literary and social issues as cogently as *The Court and the Castle*, and none is the result of more sustained thought and study. Like J. B. Priestley's vastly underrated *Literature and Western Man*, *The Court and the Castle* is the distillation of a lifetime of reading. Whereas it displays little of Priestley's astonishing memory,[1] the book is both more self-revealing and tightly organized. Going beyond ideas, it relates Rebecca West's reading to her personal life. After quoting Goethe's criticism of Hamlet in *Wilhelm Meister*, she opens a new approach to her subject by starting her next paragraph, "I then went to Skoplje, a town in Macedonia."[2] This practice of relating literature to life, although eschewed by formal criticism, gains for *The Court and the Castle* a sharp cutting edge. By telling us what kind of person she is and by frankly discussing her experiences in and out of books, Rebecca West takes hold of the reader. He knows he is going to be entertained and instructed by someone to whom literature and politics are no dry intellectual exercises. *The Court and the Castle* is a book with a bite. The richness of Rebecca West's responses and her sincere, confidential tone sustain the reader throughout.

The recurrent theme mentioned in the book's subtitle, *Some Treatments of a Recurrent Theme*, is the continuance of man through generation and organization. That man keeps his kind going by sexual reproduction and by leaguing politically may not be a new idea. But Rebecca West adds freshness and depth to it. What compels her, first of all, is the obsession of writers as different as Shakespeare, Proust, and Kafka with the fact that God has committed Himself to imperfection—sex and political agencies—to carry out His earthly plan. Just as redolent of original sin is the notion that man's private and political needs often conflict. Once again, Rebecca West cannot claim originality: Comte, Herbert Spencer, and the Auden circle in the 1930s all forecasted a political system which would yoke personal impulse to a public good. Rebecca West joins the inquiry by asking whether self-knowledge and self-being, if attainable at all, can be better reached individually or collectively. The courtier's place in the court has shifted radically over the centuries; Rebecca West shifts the terms of her argument accordingly as she moves from Shakespeare's monarchies to Kafka's welfare bureaucracies. To maintain proper balance, she will even discuss "prepolitical" writers like Joyce and Lawrence as a reminder that the courtier is never completely soluble in the court. By describing man before he is socialized, these writers show that the quick of being cannot be touched by our social arrangements.

Given the character of Rebecca West and the many years and experiences that went into the making of *The Court and the Castle*, we cannot be surprised by the power the book wields. Her rigorous reading of Hamlet's attack on his mother (act 3, sc. 4) bears out Hamlet's inadequacy as his father's avenger: "In the course of over eighty lines . . . he devotes only three to a perfunctory mention of the fact that her [Gertrude's] present husband murdered her previous husband." [3] Rebecca West is just as adroit in using evidence to prove a point as she is in collecting the evidence. Refuting the German Goethe and developing ideas stated first by the Russian Turgenev and the Spaniard de Madariaga, she integrates her own observations of Hamlet into a living tradition of Shakespeare criticism. In her view, posterity has deliberately misread Hamlet's nature because we see so much of ourselves in him and because we always want to believe the best of ourselves. Her currycombing of the play reverses posterity's decree that Hamlet could not make up his mind.

Hamlet is Shakespeare's most pessimistic play, but for reasons that oppose the hero's irresolution: far from being indecisive, Hamlet is a disobedient son, a false friend, a rash lover, and a murderer so callous that he kills men's souls along with their bodies. Another supposedly inherited fiction Rebecca West exposes concerns the death of Ophelia. And she argues so sensibly that her conclusions, no matter how maverick they may be, force us to think our way back through the play:

> The myth which has been built around Hamlet is never more perverse than when it pretends that Ophelia went mad for love and killed herself. No line in the play suggests that she felt either passion or affection for Hamlet. She never mentions him in the mad scene, and Horatio says of her, "She speaks much of her father."

Her willingness to discuss contradictory evidence strengthens Rebecca West's arguments. By dealing candidly with passages that seem to disprove her, she creates the integrity that clinches her thesis:

> For that Ophelia drowned herself is stated definitely only by two people: the clowns in the graveyard. . . . For the rest, the priest declares that "her death was doubtful" (V. 1. 228), and that the doubt was enough to make it necessary that she should be buried with "maimed rites" (V. 1. 220). But surely we are not intended to believe him, for he is drawn as a bigot, who finds it possible to answer her brother coldly when he asks, "What ceremony else?" (V. 1. 224), and it is to be presumed that such lack of charity would invent a doubt. Shakespeare will not allow anyone in the graveyard scene, even to the priest, to be without sin.

Her ability to read accurately rarely fails her. She mistakenly uses Hamlet's complaint that Claudius popped in between the election and his, Hamlet's own, hopes (act 5, sc. 2) as proof that the Danish throne was elective and not hereditary. But lapses like these are rare. Offsetting them are a wealth of rich insights. For instance, her linguistic training allows her to perceive important gradations of meaning. By combining her background in modern languages with her unifying skill, she uncovers an important religious current in the title of Proust's *A la recherche du temps perdu:*

> The word *perdu* has connotations hardly present in our word "lost," except in the expression "a lost soul." There is a suggestion of waste and ruin and despair: the great hall in French law courts where litigants wait their turn is called *la salle des pas perdus,* a dress which has been irretrievably spoiled is *perdue.*[4]

The scope and the analytical power that make up *The Court and the Castle* create an exciting mood. Although she does not always convince, she argues so nimbly and provocatively that she never lets us relax. The rousing passage can be a surprising analogy:

> What Dickens was trying to say about Bill Sikes' Nancy [in *Oliver Twist*] is very much the same thing that Dostoevsky says about Sonya Semyonovna in *Crime and Punishment.*

These analogies, while remaining within the limits of a given subject, open new possibilities. Passages like the following fan literary discussion with a cheer and freshness it often needs: "Herman Wouk's *The Caine Mutiny* . . . dealt with material which was common to Shakespeare and Conrad: with a question of keeping or breaking an oath taken to meet a danger." The refusal to distinguish between popular fiction and masterpiece universalizes her arguments. The brilliant generalization is by no means uncommon in her criticism:

> *Vanity Fair* is a masterpiece, but it is not a true satire. Neither in that book nor in any other of his writings did Thackeray attack anything which anybody would defend; and satire is essentially an attack on some person or institution or movement unworthy of the support which he or she or it is receiving from society.[5]

Most of Rebecca West's readers, however, admire the extended argumentative passage whose lucidity, close attention to details, and logical flow of idea sound a note of irresistible authority. (These brilliant arguments occur often enough to excuse omitting a long quotation.)

The technique of *The Court and the Castle* cannot be defined. Rebecca West is just as alive to literary and social history as she is to explication and comparative study. Thus she places Fielding's *Amelia* in the context of contemporary developments in trade and finance. This sure historical grasp also allows her, later in the book, to read Kafka from the standpoint of Jewish social life under the Habsburg dynasty. Her historical thrust gains power from its manysidedness and combining force. She rarely misses a chance to create either a new relationship or a new context. She thus corrects Thackeray's estimate of Fielding as a rake by using a more sophisticated biographical technique than Thackeray. Trollope's novels also emerge as outcroppings of biographical and social trends: she bases Trollope's lifelong fascination for politics and sociology (viz., the court) in his father's business failures. These failures first heaped upon Trollope the shame of going to Harrow as a charity boy and later sent him to the warmth and security of the civil service. But Rebecca West does not pretend that art is the simple product of psychological reaction. To develop the social import of Trollope's novels, she frames her psychological study with a short historical treatise on the British civil service.

Although there is no consistent method at work in *The Court and the Castle*, the book's lavish borrowings from other disciplines and its firm grounding in western tradition rule out the term, impressionistic. She has the rare critical gift of showing that literature really matters to our lives without turning literature into a self-inventory. She performs this feat by reading with the eye of an artist. Whereas her measured, formalized arguments remind one of the Henry James of the Prefaces, her freshness and vigor place her much closer to D. H. Lawrence. Like Lawrence, she responds so sharply to what she reads that she often changes, rather than interprets, it. Her version of Prospero in *The Tempest* may offend academic criticism, but academic criticism is richer for it. On the basis of his scourging of Caliban and his neglecting his bond with Ariel, Prospero is labelled a colonial imperialist in the worst sense. Her bafflment with him touches upon Renaissance social conventions: "This is strange conduct in a character who is depicted as the representative of the Renaissance intellectual, the modern artist and scholar." [6] Her ironic portrait of Prospero as a ruler corrupted by both artistic and political power not only squares well with her studies of other Shakespearean heroes. It proves that a fine critical insight can stretch the boundaries of literary scholarship. Rebecca West is right when judged by the standards of *The Court and the Castle*; she may also be right when judged by ours, should we take up her challenge.

The challenging question she asks is whether we can know or save ourselves through action. As expected, the question is put and then examined with a strong Augustinian bias. Augustine himself stands forth in the book's second paragraph as the shaping force of western literature: "It is fifteen hundred years since St. Augustine made what proved to be a rough inventory of what the literature that came after him was going to discuss." [7] The sexual symptoms of original sin pulsate forebodingly throughout. Shakespeare and Kafka, especially, knew that, while sex perpetuates life, it also corrupts and diminishes. Proust viewed sex somewhat more uneasily: whereas, along with Shakespeare and Kafka, he distrusted heterosexuality, he feared homosexuality as a public danger infecting all social institutions ranging from the family to government.

If man is stained by original sin, then both tradition, consisting of man's inherited energies, and society, consisting of collective man, must be equally stained. As soon as we act together, we pledge ourselves to imperfection. Living in society means compromise; unless our political thinking remains supple and revisionist, our laws atrophy. A man who does not compromise cannot legislate effectively. Unfortunately, compromise means giving in to badness; a political leader will misbehave in order to promote a public good. But since nobody can predict the future, his sacrifice of conscience may yield no public good. Politics creates moral chaos, especially for the ruler. The corrupting nature of power is a major theme in Shakespeare. Lear has been raised above humanity for so long by his kingly office that he can have no personal relationships. His isolation from humanity is so complete that he can only be companioned by a man wearing a disguise. The divisive nature of the throne cannot be put aside. Political law decrees unswervingly that a ruler cannot afford moral principles. Neither good nor bad, he operates alone, sacrificing both friendship and moral conduct for his subjects. Rebecca West returns to the sacrificial nature of kingship in *The Birds Fall Down*. The kingly lot of the tsars is just as lonely and wearing as that of Shakespeare's royal heroes. By making himself the testing-ground for new moralities, the king forfeits both morals and fellowship.

The nerve-tearing duties of the king create the need to formulate the basis of kingship. Since the king sacrifices and suffers so much more than anyone else in his realm, his office takes on metaphysical properties. To many, he is an absolute monarch ruling by divine right. His infallibility reveals itself in his chastisement, which he interprets as the royal privilege of joining Christ in suffering. But the principle of the divinely appointed king is by no means generally accepted. Opposing it is the principle of government by contract. As has been said, the contractual principle permits a citizenry to oust its ruler as soon as the ruler ceases to protect them. Although a monarchist, Shakespeare always worried about the split claim of kingship. The conflict between the principles of kingly rule by divine right and by contract takes away any clear title to the throne: "In play after play Shakespeare was to record his sense that monarchy is at once a necessary and dangerous institution." [8] His monarchist theme first appears in *Richard II*. The ruction at the start between Bolingbroke and Norfolk proves that the nobles of the court would destroy civic order if permitted to act freely. Unfortunately, the same royal authority that puts down revolt and maintains order also misleads the ruler into believing himself infallible. Rejecting all advice, Richard acquires an autocratic vanity that causes his downfall. His throne is then usurped by a worse man. Bolingbroke's royal actions convey starkly the truth that kings cannot conduct their business morally. For Bolingbroke violates two laws as soon as he claims the throne—the law forbidding murder and the law of dynastic succession. The nonsense public power makes of morals also stings him personally. After learning of Exton's murder of Richard, he says (act 5, sc. 6, ll. 38–40), "They love not poison that do poison need,/Nor do I thee; though I did wish him dead,/I hate the murderer, love him murdered." Great men are driven to perform public deeds they privately condemn. Bolingbroke must welcome the murder of the deposed sovereign because Richard alive would be a constant rallying point for revolt and insurrection.

But what happens when a ruler does not want to surrender his conscience to his office? Can he keep his integrity by refusing to govern? *Measure for Measure, King Lear*, and *The Tempest* all answer this question negatively. Together they agree that there is no escaping the contagion of power. The good man who shuns rule becomes both a bad man and a bad king. By shirking public duty, he makes it possible for a worse man to rule. Prospero's love of scholarship creates a royal vacuum that the wicked Antonio fills. Rebecca West interprets the withdrawal from public office in Shakespeare as a function of original sin. Nobody will deny that the job of governing a country can be morally contaminating. Yet, by reading all disavowals of action as a disavowal of action itself, Rebecca West overstates her case. Lear has for so long centered his life around a submissive court that he is no longer tethered to reality; Vincentio and Prospero, rather than turning in disgust from action as something intrinsically bad, gird themselves for action—Vincentio for the job of refurbishing the law and Prospero for the creation of art.

The usurper in Shakespeare, however, does fit the pattern of original sin. Magna Charta says that any king neglectful of his duties deserves to be deposed. In Shakespeare, too, the usurper mounts the throne because the legitimate king rules badly; his wresting of power is a public beneficence. Yet the usurper always outdoes the legitimate king in badness. Although Richard Crookback is the best example, other Shakespearean rulers bring out the evil inherent to the usurper:

Angelo is worse than Vincentio, Antonio is worse than Prospero. They are bound to be worse, because the belief that they can grow better through their own efforts encourages pride, which makes them ride roughshod over persons and principles.[9]

The king-and-usurper theme infers that man is not free to choose. That a usurper is more clever than the king he supplants is a truth that works to nobody's advantage. His added intelligence makes him capable of sinning more subtly than the deposed king, and his disrespect for the legitimacy of the throne shows him capable of sinning on a gross public scale. Nothing can be done when a king breaks public faith. As the product of human exertions, reform smacks of original sin. When a usurper assumes the throne, he attacks both the person and the office of the king. The fortunes of the realm always diminish, encouraging new usurpers and turning the court into a whispering gallery of conspirators.

The king-and-usurper theme always yields the same conclusions: that salvation is not attainable through deeds and that the courtiers are really waging their political drama in the courts of heaven. In *Hamlet*, the fact that Hamlet is neither a king nor a usurper while Claudius is both reflects the distorted state of the Danish court. In Henry James, the usurper is the upstart, the man who craves social rank but lacks the necessary social credentials. Proust's usurper, owing to sweeping changes in late nineteenth-century France, displaces an already displaced queen. In Meredith and Hardy the usurper is a woman. Rebecca West sees in these writers a wish to rebuild society along feminist lines. They constantly invented female characters whose sound, healthy instincts, if given rein, would destroy society's present arrangements. The vast superiority of these women to their men fixes woman as the true reformer of the court.

The feminism in *The Court and the Castle*, however, is muted. Its only other occurrence also treats woman's freedom. Katherine Howard and Shakespeare's Ophelia each exemplify the royal tendency to use women as political pawns. Lacking political power herself, Ophelia must first spy upon Hamlet and then listen to his obscene chatter; she would also have become Hamlet's mistress had her father thought sex politically useful to Claudius. Katherine Howard did become a sexual cipher by royal mandate. To show his good faith to Rome, Henry VIII wedded and bedded the Papist Katherine. Yet when political trends softened Henry's attitude toward Protestantism, he beheaded her. Four centuries did not enlarge woman's freedom by much. Just as the Renaissance king loved ideologies more than any wife, so did the Victorian merchant value his money more than his daughters. Trollope shows the inhumanity of barring women from ownership or inheritance. Since everything a Victorian woman owned lawfully went to her husband, the woman's father often selected that husband. The basis of the selection, of course, had little to do with the daughter's happiness. Rebecca West probably overrates Trollope. (She calls him a great novelist—better than Thackeray and as good as Dickens.) But she does well to praise him for forcing his contemporaries to look at their marriage conventions and to see what happens when marriage and family are reduced to a business deal.

Rebecca West ends *The Court and the Castle* with a long literary-historical survey of the question of choice and free will. Jane Austen's faith in the redemptive power of the will is sharply undercut by her belief that the individual and society are always at odds. Unlike Shakespeare, Jane Austen affirms the potency of action, but she favors the collective will over the private will. The courtiers must regulate their lives by the rules of the court if life is to go on:

> She did not find it intolerable that individuals should be obliged to arrive at a compromise with society and at many points, often of the greatest importance, disobey the voice of morality as they heard it and follow the pure and interested social code. Indeed to Jane Austen and to many intelligent people of her day, compromise itself was morality. . . . She must have thought of society as consisting of individuals and something else, and that something else a collective will that was working for salvation.[10]

Victorian fiction, until Meredith and Hardy, subdued the courtiers to the court, but for a different reason from Jane Austen's. Dickens, Thackeray, and Trollope were undone by

their age: all three writers subdued the artist's godlike grasp
of personal uniqueness in favor of a newly evolved social tradition that stressed the supremacy of the group. By writing
of institutions, not persons, Dickens plumps for the court;
in his work the human will attains order through group action. Ironically, his great achievement lies in his characters.
But by assuming that people take their reality from social or
industrial agencies, he fails to exploit his best gifts. His lack
of primary interest in character is seen in the flawed motivation of *Oliver Twist*, the real subject of which is the work-
house.

Thackeray betrays his preference for collective man in his
shabby treatment of "the most living of his individuals,
Becky Sharp." [11] Angry that Becky flouts social convention
so well, he makes her do things inconsistent with her basic
nature in order to have an excuse for punishing her. This
same extroversion dictates his dismissal of *Vanity Fair* as a
puppet show. Trollope's preference for the court, as has been
mentioned, inhered in his father's failure and disgrace.
Trollope saw society as an imperfect network of pegs and
holes: because the pegs outnumbered the holes, some of the
leftover pegs had to be ignored. Since people are basically
selfish, they cannot be trusted to balance the unfair ratio between pegs and holes. The job can only be done by large social organizations. Hence Trollope's lifelong obsession with
public institutions and administrative reform. He knows
these agencies, like Hiram's Hospital in *The Warden*, to be
imperfect, but he also knows that the imperfection cannot
usually be scotched without annihilating the public service
altogether:

> Trollope shows us how true it may be that institutions
> founded in the past cannot be kept alive without injustice
> to the present, yet must be preserved, since even when an
> institution operates without full regard to the rights of any
> section of the community, the people in that section may
> be the worse off if the institution should collapse alto-
> gether, because they will lose the partial regard it accorded
> their rights. Trollope had a great understanding of the
> morphology of society.[12]

Trollope's belief that the individual takes his value from his niche in the social hierarchy saves the individual from becoming a social discard. But it also diminishes him. For if Trollope understood the structure of society, he knew little about the substance. His characters have so little life apart from their social relationships that they materialize as puppets. Trollope's obsession with the court drained the blood from his courtiers. Having been shaped to the pattern of society, they exist only socially.

Like Trollope, Proust lived in an era of great social change. Both writers were as familiar with the usurper figure as Shakespeare. But the increasing complexity of society increased the number of usurpers: instead of residing with a monarch, power was strewn among legislative cabinets, the civil service, the popular press, the landed gentry, and the new merchant-industrialist class. A capitalist democracy not only scatters power; it also makes the corrupting effects of power more contagious. In Proust, everybody is dirtied by the Dreyfus case. Now that public power has passed from a central authority to a legislature both elected and staffed by the public, the public must bear the guilt for its country's crimes.

Responsibility in a democratic bureaucracy is a subject of special interest to Kafka. As a civil servant, Kafka paints a more intimate picture than Proust of the inner mechanism of society. Society in Kafka has grown so crowded that it can only be organized by a vast, complex impersonal machinery. Kafka's worry is not that man and society have different aims. What haunts him is that the corporate will has grown so inscrutable that it must summon a nonexistent law to execute an innocent man for having performed an unknown crime. Yet, in the name of social necessity, Kafka accepts his democratic bureaucracy just as Shakespeare accepted the monarchy—as "beneficent, comic, absolutely necessary and murderously cruel." [13] With no supreme authority to compel civil obedience in times of emergency, a democracy must use indirect tactics. If the tactics are macabre and mad, they nevertheless complete a circuit with what is macabre and mad in human nature. The argument over free will has come back to the quarrel between Bolingbroke and Norfolk in the first scene of *Richard II*. It has also come back to the question of original sin. Is it a sign of our fallen state that we can only survive by pressing into service ugliness and cruelty? Rebecca West's next two books, A Train of Powder and The New Meaning of Treason, join the issue of man's self-perpetuation. By moving the basis of her inquiry from literature to the law, she both reshapes her inquiry and subjects it to the test of democratic process in the postwar western world.

A Train of Powder and The New Meaning of Treason contain the essays that have placed Rebecca West in the company of the century's best political journalists. Whereas her standing as a novelist and literary critic is unsure, her work as a journalist is universally admired. Here is Kenneth Tynan voicing a typical attitude: "Rebecca West is still the best journalist alive, the only one who can record both the facts and their flavour without loss of grace or vigour." [14] Written as reports of notable postwar trials, these magazine essays reflect our age's fascination for courtroom procedures. Inherit the Wind and Anatomy of a Murder are but two items in a slew of films, novels, plays, and television series that have tapped the dramatic resources of legal process. Another contemporary feature of these books is their premise that our world is breaking into pieces. Like Neville Chamberlain before him, General Howley, the American commandant of Berlin in the late 1940s, learned that the western democracies were faced with men who do not keep their word. The defunct world is that of the gentlemanly officer and the businessman who abides by the trust inhering in the credit system. Traditionless, Hitler and Stalin hold no truck with this world. The traitor, whom Rebecca West studies as an evolving incarnation in The New Meaning of Treason, has further despoiled honor and decency, forcing the creation of massive bureaucracies like the ones in Kafka.

A Train of Powder contains six essays written between 1946 and 1954, four of which first appeared in The New Yorker. Although the book was not planned as a unified work, it still coheres thematically. The epigraph, taken from John Donne, gives it both its title and its metaphysical focus:

Our God is not out of breath, because he hath blown one tempest, and swallowed a Navy: our God hath not burnt out his eyes, because he hath looked upon a Train of Powder.

The dominant mood of A *Train of Powder* is one of darkness. The collapse of the basis virtues of decency and honor is only one symptom of the general breakdown. Modern life has grown so disoriented that nothing is as it seems. Often, justice cannot even be carried out:

> It was a very ordinary story. What made it extraordinary was that, though everybody who knew him [Brian Donald Hume], including his wife, to whom he was a devoted husband, believed it, not a word of it was true.

> It was so little surprising that [William] Marshall had landed in the dock that it was very surprising.[15]

How can one get on with life when all certainties have disappeared? None of the trials in A *Train of Powder* releases a clear meaning or traces a neat pattern. Murderers are still at large without having been tried, and traitors have destroyed elaborate security precautions without having been detected. To use a familiar contrast in Rebecca West, the Nuremberg war trials, the Greenville, South Carolina, lynching trial of 1947, the Setty murder trial of 1950, and the Kuznetsov-Marshall espionage case of 1952 are all events that never become experiences. It is a sign of our helplessness that the mass of facts connected with these cases have not taught us to cope better with reality. Yet it is also a sign that there is more to life than facts. These four trials, while trampling orthodox jurisprudence, affirm life's ability to go on. The choice of Donne as the presiding spirit of the book gives man's endurance a theological thrust. In line with Rebecca West's religious attitude, which is strongly pre-Vatican II in spirit, God's grace outruns all human energies—even those given over to self-destruction. As in *The Court and the Castle*, the action in A *Train of Powder* goes on in the courts of heaven.

In her 1952 essay, "Goodness Doesn't Just Happen," Rebecca West establishes personal liberty as the goal of civilization. The law serves this goal by making sure that one person's freedom does not interfere with that of another:

I see the main problem of my life, and indeed anybody's life, as the balancing of competitive freedom. . . . a sense of mutual obligations that have to be honored, and a legal system which can be trusted to step in when that sense fails.[16]

The law, then, is the regulating agency of civilized process; it both defines and defends the boundaries of civilized conduct. Theoretically, it should only have to be summoned when the codes of love, friendship, and honor fail. As such, it is the last brake to violence. Yet, as much as she dislikes violence, Rebecca West does not subordinate the individual to the law. Her appreciation of both the sacredness and the uniqueness of persons is seen in the methodology of A Train of Powder and The New Meaning of Treason. She will always try to establish a human reference for public events. Like Carlyle and Macaulay, she humanizes her documentaries by treating them as biography whenever she can. On the other hand, she appreciates vividly those legal and civic arrangements which give personality, the core of biography, its chance for self-expression.

Rebecca West is richly endowed with the reporter's gift of selecting from a swarm of persons and events the ones that best serve her purpose. This skill marks the chief difference between her technique-ridden early novels and her high journalism. Her natural bent is not one of inventiveness, but of observation, interpretation, and synthesis. Her imagination works best on something already there—an idea, a witness's testimony, or a social event. Working with a given seems to guide—regulating rather than restraining—her creativity. Art is rigorously selective, but court reporting, like the law itself, always welcomes new evidence. An abundance of facts is more apt to produce a just verdict than a smattering; so while the novelist must guard against cluttering his work with data, the juror craves information of all kinds.

Another big difference between the early fiction and the court journalism resides in tone. Rebecca West does not write self-consciously in A Train of Powder or The New Meaning of Treason. She treads the common ground of public events and does so with a thoroughness and a practicality that appeals to the reader's common sense. The tone of these works suggest that, instead of uncovering new terrain, she prefers to comb already trodden ground. Her working premise that civilization bears heavily on the effectiveness of the law creates a straightforward, workmanlike rhetoric. Like her rhetoric, her morality is grounded in sharable, not arcane, experience. She is trying to address as wide an audience as possible on subjects of major public importance. Hence, anything that makes life more pleasant and coherent gains her hearty support: "Harry Collins believed in bringing coal out of the ground, no matter whether the ground was British or American or French or German, because coal is a good thing for human beings to have about the place." Accordingly, Rebecca West uses familiar items, homey analogies, and anecdotes about common subjects to foster a community of fellowship between herself and the reader:

> One could not buy a new hat, a new kettle, a yard of ribbon, a baby's diaper. There was no money, there were only cigarettes.

> She . . . is a topographical photographer of high professional standing, and writes travel books which bring the story back complete with its tail feathers.

> He asked the court to clear a high hurdle. . . . It was quite impossible to swallow Marshall's story.[17]

Sometimes, these strolls through the human landscape yield precious gems. Instead of fabricating a rich, brocaded effect, Rebecca West's journalism unearths richness in the soil of ordinary experience. She collects and assembles her materials with a sure polemical instinct. Often, she will tell or remind us of the outcome of a trial early in her essay in order to sharpen her picture of the steps by which the outcome was reached. The technique of blunting suspense also enlarges the human drama, accentuating the laws, issues, and institutions at stake during the trial.

Technique blends into wisdom at the end of her report on

the Nuremberg trials. After clearing the court, she offers a brief historical survey of techniques of capital punishment. The survey shows legal history streaked with blood and scored with the cries of the executed. But rather than ending on this sentimental note, Rebecca West introduces the names of William Marwood and James Berry. These obscure Victorians (Marwood was an unlettered Lincolnshire cobbler) were great humanitarians, and Rebecca West discusses their humanitarian experiments with trapdoors and ropes of different length to prevent hanged men from strangling to death. Thus the essay achieves both a surprise and a moral climax in its closing pages. To claim greatness for Marwood and Berry is to claim greatness for mercy. Yet, Rebecca West's admiration for ordinary life need not be grounded in specific achievements. In what seem digressions, she uncovers the things people live by—what they love and how they work. Work is especially redeeming, and she salutes those who do their jobs creatively. Even justice is better served because a charwoman can distinguish between the sounds produced by a Hoover and an Electrolux vacuum cleaner.

Rebecca West both extends civilized process and applies it to herself by shrinking from detached intellectual relationships. As part of her investigations, she will visit the bunker where Hitler was killed or take a punting trip along the Essex marshland to the place where a corpse was discovered. Often she will use contrast, not only as a rhetorical device, but as a means of infusing her argument with as much data as she can. If the added data makes adjudication more difficult, it also promotes justice. Speaking of the staggering amount of time, energy, and legal skill that went into the Nuremberg trials, she insists, "we went to war to preserve such pernicketiness." [18] Contrast still seems to be her favorite way of making the reader understand the value of civilized process. Thus "Mr. Setty and Mr. Hume" opens, "The murder of Mr. Setty was important, because he was so unlike the man who found his headless and legless body," and "Opera in Greenville" combines on its first page the clean, sparkling water that refreshes Greenville and the city's oppressive heat.[19]

The web of contrasts that opens the first essay in the book is more elaborate. Rebecca West takes hold of the reader straightaway by creating the impression that "the world's enemy," as yet unnamed, is charging at him. Yet before the sentence ends, the note of danger and the impressionistic technique that sounded the note have both vanished. The enemy hardly seems dangerous; a danger would not be inhabiting a realm redolent of candy cane, gingerbread, and nursery tales,

> pine woods on little hills, grey-green glossy lakes, too small ever to be anything but smooth . . . russet-roofed villages with headlong gables and pumpkin-steeple churches that no architect over seven could have designed.

The second sentence probes the danger further, but again mood and sense seem askew: "Another minute and the plane dropped to the heart of the world's enemy: Nuremberg." The quiet, even tone holds as we are gently led into the flaming quick—the courtroom where the Nazi war criminals are being tried in the most spectacular international trial of the century. The prevailing mood of boredom is finally accounted for in the last sentence of the paragraph—suitably, by means of another striking contrast:

> Some of those present were fiercely desiring that the tedium should come to an end at the first possible moment, and the others were as fiercely desiring that it should last for ever and ever.[20]

This stagnancy and stalemate sets the mood for the stellar actor in the three essays on postwar Germany—death. Death is the condition of the trial. In a ravaged Nuremberg landscape, the murderers of millions are struggling to delay their own deaths. Defendants, prosecutors, guards, reporters, interpreters, visitors, and the vanquished Nurembergers are all locked in the death-clamp of food rationing and travel restriction. What the trial will establish is the legal guilt of persons who obey unjust commands. So while a yawn symbolizes Nuremberg, the overhanging boredom did not prevent the trial's becoming a major cultural landmark. History may prove Rebecca West a prophet for making Nuremberg the cornerstone of postwar Western Civilization.

Her fine-tempered integrity never rings more purely than in her resistance to simplified moralities. She presents Nuremberg as a halfway house. Although officially at peace, the world, especially Germany, was still hemmed in by civic restraints befitting war. The Nazi prisoners were not simply bad men, the allies were not simply good men, and the will of God was not plain. Göring was denied Holy Communion by the Lutheran chaplain the night before his execution, the acquitted prisoners were abused, and the eleven hanged Nazis did not benefit from the reforms of Marwood and Berry. One man tossed and struggled for twenty minutes before choking to death. The trial and everything connected with it was a turmoil of divided aims. The Russian delegates were so set on convicting the prisoners that they lost face with their fellow prosecutors. But the defense displayed an equal measure of dissension and ignorance, their worst howler perhaps being the failure of their lawyers to learn British and American jurisprudence.

These mistakes and oversights impede justice. From its indirect invocation of theme at the outset, the essay hints at the epic. But how can ignorance, cruelty, and red tape inaugurate a civilization? How does Nuremberg qualify as a cultural landmark? Rebecca West's answer is that Nuremberg proved the supremacy of the moral will of the West. Although nobody wanted the trials to take place, all agreed that there was no alternative. So great was the need for justice that it was better that the trials be conducted badly than not a all. This attitude is not defeatist. For Nuremberg could not have been handled more smoothly. Nobody could apply precedents to Nuremberg because nothing like Nuremberg had happened before. Rebecca West's comments on the four-power control of Berlin apply just as neatly to the trials: "Let none mock at such disorganization. No great international event can be efficiently organized. There are conceivable feats of coordination which are beyond performance." [21] Although it would have been easier to settle our political accounts with the Third Reich by decree, the democratic West took the trouble to implement a clumsy, costly machinery. This capacity for extra trouble in the name of justice is what democracy is about.

Rebecca West goes on to make Nuremberg important for what it was, its character, as well as for what it meant or did. Instead of documenting local conditions, she shows what it is like to live with them. At times, she nearly becomes the homesick American GI on guard duty, the bored judge, or the visitor caught in a dispute between the civilian and military personnel attached to the court. Inside the Palace of Justice, she reviews the defendants, their place in the Nazi command, and the figures they cut at the trial. Rudolph Hess, Hitler's former personal secretary, is "plainly mad": "He looked as if his mind had no surface, as if every part of it had been blasted away except the depth where the nightmares live." Göring, too, is of a piece with his official deeds:

> He was so very soft. Sometimes he wore a German Air Force uniform, and sometimes a light beach suit in the worst of playful taste, and both hung loosely on him, giving him the air of pregnancy. He had . . . the coarse bright skin of an actor who has used grease paint for decades, and the preternaturally deep wrinkles of the drug addict. It added up to something like the head of a ventriloquist's dummy. He looked infinitely corrupt.[22]

Although defeated and denatured, the prisoners occasioned some surprise in the dock. After the acquittal of Hjalmar Schacht, former Reichsbank president, we eagerly await judgment on the more spectacular Nazis—Göring, Goebbels, and Hess. But it turns out that we are not through with Schacht after all. An orange brings him back to us. While court had adjourned for the noon break, the prisoners each got a box lunch including an orange. Unlike the other acquitted Nazis, Schacht refused to give his orange as a token of sympathy to one of his convicted friends. The orange teaches us a good deal about the order of human events. But it would have been lost to us without Rebecca West's sharp eye and dramatic instinct. Here is the godlike love of common experience she mentioned as the novelist's major trait in *The Court and the*

Castle. By noting the minor detail, she first corrects the out-sider's untutored view of legal process and then shows that process as a living organism. The tensions in the courtroom lay outside the scope of those personally unacquainted with capital trials. What seems a non sequitur is often a logical outgrowth of the trial. Many visitors recoiled when the pris-oners laughed at the German pronunciation of the American and British court officers. The dynamics of the trial explain, though, that the prisoners had earned a right to laugh. One need not go to literature for black humor:

> That is something pitiable which those who do not attend trials never see: the eagerness with which people in the dock snatch at any occasion for laughter. . . . These de-fendants laughed when they could, and retained their com-posure when it might well have cracked.[23]

Rebecca West used one of her free moments to visit a greenhouse. Her first surprise lay in seeing the greenhouse so clean and so well stocked with flourishing cyclamens. But more surprising was the man who grew the cyclamens—a one-legged, middle-aged man who could not stoop and bend, as gardeners must, without chancing danger. The cyclamen, a perennial bloom, furnishes the title of Rebecca West's three essays on postwar Germany (1946, 1949, 1954). The hobbling gardener becomes a metaphor of his blasted country. At first, Rebecca West explains him as a sign of energy and renewal. But she changes her mind: doing only one thing, regardless of the deed, is not the same as conducting a process. Marc Sallafranque's bubbling good will played just as large a part in his commercial success in *The Thinking Reed* as his will-power. Tenacity marks the drill sergeant, not the general. The cyclamen-grower is so driven by his ruling passion that he has bypassed the lesson of Nuremberg: that endurance must fuse with sanity and life before it can aid civilization.

The 1949 essay carries forward the argument of the cycla-mens and their grower. Germany has changed since the trials. Postwar reconstruction, having moved its focus outside the courtroom, now takes on the character of a full-scale drama: "Interest comes when people start to act out an idea, to show what a thought is worth when it is worked out in flesh and blood." [24] Whereas Nuremberg showed men debating justice formally, the later essay shows women joining the debate with their bodies as well as their minds. The quadripartite control of Berlin, while politically necessary, created such logistical problems that reconstruction nearly collapsed at the outset. As in Nuremberg, everybody in Berlin and Hamburg in 1949 was a prisoner. None of the four controlling powers could recall their forces lest the other three take their withdrawal as a sign of military weakness. But the chief obstacle to a crisp, clean-run reconstruction was war itself. With her usual generosity, Rebecca West reminds us that the job of feeding, housing and restoring to work several million people cannot be done in a humane, orderly way. But rather than bemoaning the fact, she stresses the honest endeavor that went into rebuilding Germany's economy. The war did not bring out the worst in everybody. Although some refused to make sacrifices, others acted with surprising nobility. The contribution of these people was heroic. Without their patience and moral grit, Germany would have remained a shambles for many years.

"Greenhouse with Cyclamens III" is a much more theoretical and restrospective study. Written eight years after Nuremberg, it owes its life to two events—Rebecca West's trip to Geneva for an international congress of economists and the publication of *The Sword in the Scales* by Hans Fritzsche, Goebbels's radio chief during the Third Reich. One of the acquitted Nazi leaders at Nuremberg, Fritzsche attacked the trials on the grounds of arbitrariness and mismanagement. Rebecca West again grants that the trials did not flow smoothly. Yet she also mentions the overriding necessity of forging a legal instrument by which to judge the Nazis. The eight intervening years have not changed her opinion that the trials had to be held for the sake of reason and love. But has the world profited from Nuremberg? When brought to the test of action, has Nuremberg encouraged civilized values? Rebecca West answers these questions guardedly but optimistically. Although she musters no statistics, she points to a thriving West Germany. West Germany's rejection of communism and her membership in the Geneva conference signals the coming of a new moral order.

"Opera in Greenville," which reports the South Carolina trial of thirty-one white men accused of lynching a Negro in February, 1947, again shows justice vindicated at an awful cost. Like the Nazi convicts at Nuremberg, the jailer holding the Negro in custody was told by a powerful authority to commit a crime—that of surrendering his prisoner. Also like Nuremberg, Greenville was a collective trial. But instead of being sentenced, the Greenville defendants were all acquitted. "Opera in Greenville" has a special value. As usual, Rebecca West conveys the personality of the court, the town, and the times. But she also reasons with a lucidity beyond the powers of most Americans. (On issues like racial violence and federal intervention, we are too easily stung to muster cool, balanced judgments.) Aside from showing us how we look to an outsider, she fits the lynching trial into a spectrum of legal tradition. Her ability to avoid rancor merges nicely with her journalistic craving for facts. Supremely fair, she investigates those social truths that bear on the case not only legally, but also dramatically. Details of local architecture, statements from FBI records, and personal interviews all get into her report. But so does less technical data. She begins by taking Greenville, South Carolina, on its own terms; as the boldest thing about the town is its fierce heat, she discusses it in her first paragraph. One of her most humane traits over the years has been her charitable outlook on human endeavor: while having learned not to ask too much of people, she warmly appreciates all expressions of kindness and good sense. Given the heat, the time of night, and the remoteness of the town jail, she pardons the jailer who turned Willie Earle over to the lynching mob. Repeatedly, she persuades us by personal example that knowledge and generosity go hand in hand. Her compassion, her exhaustive research, and her zest for legal process describe a master jurist better than a journalist.

The word "Opera" in the title of the essay refers to the bombast and fustian that mark much of southern life. But instead of attacking or patronizing this overstatedness, Rebecca West accepts it. The solid accomplishments of the natives of Greenville outweigh any folk eccentricities: "To sustain the life of a large modern city in this cloying, clinging heat is an amazing achievement." [25] To give substance to her admiration, she mentions that the main hotel in Greenville is both cleaner and more comfortable than the world-renowned hotels in New York and that, despite its heat, Greenville keeps the same business hours as New York. Rebecca West praises when it would be easier to condemn. Like any good juror, she does not go to court with her mind already made up.

Her immersion in the subculture of the Greenville taxi driver has a powerful effect on the reader. Her detailed, sympathetic account insures us that, while important legal questions are at stake, the Greenville case partakes basically of sweat, muscle, and bone. A community where few own cars and where most prefer to travel at night, owing to the heavy daytime heat, will need a large cadre of night-riding taxi drivers. To cap her short sociological study of local traffic conditions, Rebecca West offers a brilliant summary of the Greenville taxi drivers:

> The taxi drivers of Greenville are drawn from the type of men who drive taxis anywhere. They are people who dislike steady work in a store or a factory or an office, or have not the aptitude for it, have a certain degree of mechanical intelligence, have no desire to rise very far in the world, enjoy driving for its own sake, and are not afraid of the dangers that threaten those who are on the road at night. They are, in fact, tough guys.[26]

The dangers of driving at night into Negro neighborhoods, where the taxi drivers are disliked, cannot be exaggerated. And the drivers know it. They have often raised money by claiming to have been beaten and robbed by their Negro fares. But neither can the Negroes of Greenville claim moral superiority. They too have used the taxis to whet racial prejudice. An interview with a prominent local Negro explains that, in spite of warnings by leading fellow citizens, Greenville Negroes cannot resist the temptation of paying a white man to do a job.

None of this ferment was put to rest by the trial. In the

first place, the trial should have been held outside of Greenville; since the jurors were townsmen of the taxi drivers, it
would have been difficult for them to return a verdict of
guilty. The machinery of the trial, like its setting, augured no
good: "The trial had not the pleasing pattern, the agreeable
harmony and counterpoint, of good legal process." [27] Of special regret was the attorneys' blatant contempt for the jury.
By invoking scripture, by exaggerating their southern accents,
and by faulting the federal government for meddling in local
affairs, counsel played upon the jurors' narrowest prejudices.
This demagoguery drew frequent rebukes from the bench,
as one would hope. The baseness of the demagoguery shows
through in Rebecca West's valuation of one of the defense
attorney's arguments: "A more disgusting incident cannot
have happened in any court of law at any time." [28] Yet despite this underhandedness, the Greenville lynching trial sent
out several bright rays of hope. Rebecca West's final judgment of the proceedings raises the law to a category of meta-
physics: justice works, but in ways neither clear nor satisfying
to the reason. She reacts first to the acquittal of the thirty-one
taxi drivers by lamenting that the central moral issue of the
trial was ignored. By forgetting that murder cannot be par-
doned in a civilized society, the citizens of Greenville betrayed themselves. But whereas the trial taught Greenville
nothing, it exerted a civilizing force that touched Greenville
afterwards. Reviewing her 1947 report of the trial, Rebecca
West notes in 1954 an absence of lynching crimes in the
southern United States for the past three years. Although
never officially vindicated, by 1954 the law had gauged the
less formal but more cogent requirements of daily life in the
South. As in Nuremberg, people in Greenville began discovering the law for themselves by working out its claims in
sweat and muscle.

Faith in both the law and people characterizes "Mr. Setty
and Mr. Hume," the report of a 1950 murder trial held in
London. The trial of Brian Donald Hume, a commercial pilot
and small suburban shopkeeper, tells a cruel, somber story.
Stanley Setty, born in Baghdad in 1903, was an undischarged
bankrupt without a bank account or an office. Yet his forays

into that grey area "where the legitimate and the illegitimate are mingled" [29] earned for this used-car dealer and curbside banker 50,000 pounds. In the fall of 1949 he vanished. His disappearance remains a mystery; his murderers are still at large; his head and legs have never been found. The only reliable evidence pertaining to his death is his dismembered torso and the man who dumped it from his airplane into an Essex marsh. Like the other legal actions reported in *A Train of Powder*, Hume's trial was disorderly. The cases for both the defense and the prosecution were destroyed, ironically, by too much evidence. The heaped-up testimony would not cohere: "The case was all sewed up, except that the murder could not have possibly been committed in this way." [30]

This choking abundance and incoherence create the condition of the Hume-Setty trial: death. The case has a grisly unity. The presiding judge, Sir Wilfred Lewis, took fatally sick during the trial, and the wife of one of the leading witnesses died shortly before Setty's murder, perhaps even while Setty's murder was being planned. Lewis's replacement, Christmas Humphreys, and the defendant, Brian Donald Hume, embody two elements of the destructive male principle. Judge Humphreys is an enemy of reality because he has rejected the realities his society lives by:

> Mr. Humphreys is a fastidious person who is displeased with what man has made of the earth, and has therefore always distrusted the common practices of mankind. . . . Ballet is not ordinary motion, therefore he adored it; prose is more habitually used than poetry, therefore he wrote poetry and read it aloud. . . . He would have nothing to do with the Christianity which lay at his hand shaped for the use of his western personality, he insisted on going out of Europe into Asia to find a religion.[31]

Hume too thwarts life by paring away and refining out of existence crude, everyday reality: "Hume spoke with the voice that denies." [32] During the Second War, he rejected the substance of a family and a steady job in favor of the shadow of masquerading as an RAF officer. His room, no less than Judge Humphreys' religious and aesthetic preferences, bespeaks a loathing for earthly ties. The pictures thronging his walls leap violently into a mad psychological study. Just as St. Augustine could never love his mother until she was dead, Hume could not abide human flesh until its stench was whipped away by the pure, clean air of flight:

> He too had his religion. . . . That was to be seen in his apartment, which was a temple of flight. The upper parts of all the walls were obsessionally covered with photographs of planes, of aviators, of air battles, with parts of planes. . . . They were arranged in a pattern like the outline of a great bird with wings. This was not planned; it was an achievement of the daemon within Hume, who had ideas about flight beyond the sphere of aeronautics, who allowed, indeed, some pictures on his walls which were neither of planes nor aviators, which were of birds with strong wings, wild swans, wild geese, creatures of dazzling plumage, cleaving air so high and pure that it is not air at all.[33]

This air-washed bloodlessness does not drive from the court the whiff of good arable earth. For Mrs. Hume stands as staunchly behind life as her husband does behind vacancy and nothingness. Driven by a warm, abiding belief that life must be lived, she subdues everything else to the business of making a pleasant home for herself and her baby:

> She was a troubling figure to anybody who had begun to doubt the value of life as a thing in itself, who had decided that life ought to be rejected if it were this and not that. . . . She meant life to go on, whatever it was like.[34]

Other witnesses display this same reverence for life. Natural instinct wins over intellectual refinements and escapist fantasies, for the ordinary always provokes more wonder than the rare in "Mr. Setty and Mr. Hume." But the essay, together with "The Better Mousetrap," (1952) are the most restive in the book. "The Better Mousetrap," in fact, instead of rejoicing in the commonplace, finds the commonplace so balky that it rouses fear. The essay deals with the trial of William Martin Marshall, a twenty-four-year-old telegraphist for the British diplomatic service. Marshall was charged with violating the Official Secrets Act by conspiring with Pavel Kuznetsov, the second secretary of the Russian embassy in London. Like the Setty-Hume trial, the action against Marshall bulged with information. But Marshall's mind was so simple that it proved more baffling than that of an able veteran spy. So strong is Rebecca West's loathing of treason that only by desexing Marshall can she adequately express her contempt: "he had sloping shoulders, sloping as steeply as the shoulders of any Gainsborough beauty, at an angle not often seen in the male physique." [35]

The running metaphor of the embassy as a mousetrap takes us back to the Kafka territory. Rebecca West has always distrusted embassies because, like imperialist colonies and occupation armies, they put their personnel in an unfamiliar climate, where people speak an unfamiliar language and observe unfamiliar customs. Process between the individual and his environment is abolished. This undermining of process has grown starker in the postwar world. Cruel and claustrophobic, embassies now prove their effectiveness by destroying their personnel. Kuznetsov, a skilled and valued servant of long standing, was sacrificed to a secret espionage maneuver. Nothing else explains the infallible stupidity with which he conducted his meeting with Marshall. By defying both his instinct for survival and his professional training, he did all he could to deliver Marshall to British Intelligence. His bizarre assignment compels some of Rebecca West's best writing. Here is her summary and climax:

> As Kuznetsov must have noticed long before, Marshall was constitutionally unfit for underground work. Yet on June 13 the two men met at a trysting place which was even more exposed than the Normandie and Canbury Gardens, which could have been chosen, surely, only by someone who was saying, "Take him. Oh, will you never take him? Take him, take him now." [36]

What rankles here is Russia's willingness to sacrifice Kuznetsov. That he acted as a decoy is almost certain, for an obscure cub like Marshall could hardly merit the attention of a trusted professional. Sacrificed Kuznetsov was. He was sent from England in angry haste, as if he had committed a serious diplomatic error rather than following diplomatic instructions. The official anger that marked his exit from England, however, touches upon more than deportation. Because the fiction of his misconduct was so important to Soviet policy, it had to be kept up even after his return to Russia. Kuznetsov, therefore, had to be punished just as if he had committed a serious crime. This diplomatic strategy of murdering one's best officers in exchange for a faithful, workmanlike job is one dead end of espionage. Another lies in the undiscovered Soviet spy in whose behalf Kuznetsov diverted the attention of British Intelligence. The last sentence of "The Better Mousetrap" has a thin, bitter flavor that conveys the recalcitrance of the trial:

> It can be said of this larger mystery only what can be said of the lesser mystery in which William Martin Marshall was involved: the facts admit of several interpretations.[37]

This weak ending is justified. Rebecca West cannot be asked to solve the case or to give it a pleasing shape when both Scotland Yard and British jurisprudence failed. Although *A Train of Powder* does not end in brightness, the scraps of light that flash above Nuremberg, Greenville, and London reflect Rebecca West's refusal to embrace a cheap optimism. *A Train of Powder* maintains its moral balance. It searches bravely for hope in areas where negativity holds sway. But while it fends off the dead hand of negativity, it does not misread reality to suit its needs.

The New Meaning of Treason is a revision and expansion of Rebecca West's 1947 book, *The Meaning of Treason*. In contrast to *A Train of Powder*, it deals with trials not widely publicized at the time they took place. Again, the drama of the courtroom stirs her best journalistic efforts. She quotes the law: she traces it historically: she delights in the brand of it practiced by the judges at William Joyce's trial in 1946: "It was . . . as good entertainment as first-class tennis." [38] This élan also marks her response to the deeper reverberations of legal process. She reveals the law as imperfect; never

having been definitively analyzed and formulated, it sometimes parts company with facts. Unable to keep up with
social changes, which usually occur unpredictably, it is often
too conservative. Channeled through personalities, it occasionally works unfairly. Yet she does not despair. A free society can always refurbish its institutions. The trial of Joyce
is an example of the law's power of self-renewal. The outcome of the trial weighed heavily upon the status of passports, a subject the law had never before clearly defined. Rebecca West helps correct the oversight by giving a pocket
history of passports, on the basis of which she shows the law
refreshing and bolstering itself. The law can only overcome
its weaknesses by facing up to them. This self-concept of the
law as a progressive integration affirms the law as a civilizing
force. Treason, on the other hand, as a denial of process,
gives Rebecca West the sharp contrast she often invokes as a
working principle. Treason adds nothing to the world's store
of knowledge or of joy. It is an attack on one's nation, one's
countrymen, and oneself. But it can never be erased completely, even by a maturing, self-integrating discipline like
the law. Since the will to death is as basic as the will to life,
traitors will always emerge.

Like that of Brian Donald Hume, the trial of William
Joyce surprised everybody in the court by suddenly falling
into a legal deadlock: "It seemed as impossible to convict
William Joyce as it had been . . . to imagine his acquittal." [39] Here is the reason for the deadlock: British law deems
anybody a traitor who becomes a naturalized citizen of a
country at war with England. But, even though England and
Germany were enemies when Joyce offered his services to
Hitler, he believed himself no traitor. Technically, argued
defense counsel, Joyce was innocent because he was not a
British subject when he migrated to Germany and joined the
Nazi propaganda service. Rebecca West applauds the court's
handling of this legal problem. Echoing a major idea of *The
Court and the Castle,* she reminds us that any state protects
its citizens in exchange for obedience and trust. This governmental process undergirds all written law. It also decrees
that a traitor must be dealt with more harshly than an in-

vader: governments must discourage treason, since it is so difficult to detect and so harmful to public morale. Joyce enjoyed the protection of the crown during the thirty years he lived in England or carried an English passport. He thus owed the crown an acquired loyalty just as binding as the one imposed by citizenship.

The essay on Joyce, the best in the book, gains much of its drive through its deft organization. In the opening sections, Rebecca West keeps narrowing Joyce's range of legal recourse. Yet he keeps escaping the death sentence as he moves from the Old Bailey to the Court of Appeals. But midway through the essay, Rebecca West stops building suspense. On the contrary, by reminding us that Joyce, or Lord Haw-Haw, was sentenced and then hanged for broadcasting Nazi propaganda, she demolishes it. She does not shape her essay to gain a climax of event or emotion. Instead, she violates chronology to clarify the processes—legal, historical, and moral—that define Joyce's guilt. Treachery thereby becomes a political and cultural reality. What emerges from "The Revolutionary" is the principle that nations must be governed by laws, not men. Rebecca West's detachment does not dwarf Joyce's humanity. Joyce compels her admiration for bearing himself bravely while the judge pronounced the death sentence on him. Yet, we are reminded, this remarkable bravery did not raise him above his fellows. Everybody in England faced death with just as strong a heart during the six years of World War II, and some of these stronghearted souls died without having had Joyce's opportunity for legal redress. When placed alongside this extended drama of national bravery, which he bitterly mocked, Joyce hardly ranks as a martyr.

But he would not have balked at his lot in any case. William Joyce belongs to a class of traitors, now extinct, that chose treason as their means of political self-expression. Joyce saw himself as a man of mission. Insisting that he loved England, he believed her interests could best be served under the rule of Hitler. Treachery gave him the chance to broadcast his creed. His trial and the elaborate arrangements leading to it confirmed his sense of destiny; this ill-made, undersized gutter rat, who could never hold public office in a sane community, died for an ideal. Nobody could laugh at him any more. That he could only gain an audience by betraying them mattered less to him than his need for self-expression. His sacrifice ended his obscurity. The willingness to die for his political beliefs and the great attention lavished upon him after his repatriation confirmed his supreme importance.

The goals of the Fascist spy of World War II resemble those of the Communist spy of the cold war. As servants of death, fascism and communism are both natural enemies of democratic government. Democracy fosters a fluid interchange among its citizens: fascism and communism deny their subjects the freedom of choice. Rejecting nationalism, they are international; the international, conspiratorial, totalitarian nature of both creeds declares itself, first, in the Stalin-Hitler pact of 1939 and, then, in their common insistence that party loyalty overrides national loyalty, even to the extent of committing treason.

Political changes, however, have changed the traitor. Although his aims are the same as those of the Fascist spy—to break public morale and to steal restricted information—the Communist infiltrator uses more sophisticated methods. In 1933 Rebecca West brushed a raw nerve ending in our social tissue that the Communist spy was later to twitch mercilessly: "The advance of science," she observed, "must mean a certain loss to humanity as a whole; for the further it goes the further it withdraws a certain number of first-rate minds from contact with the common mind." [40] Modern society has boxed itself in. It has become so large and sprawling that it summons more and more scientific apparatus for the purpose of organizing itself. That is, it promotes the incoherence it is trying to offset. The modern state can only be run by a bureaucracy of experts, and the computer techniques used by the bureaucrats demand an enlarging force of clerks and mechanics. Security is thus imperiled; there are more secret documents and more people given access to the places where the documents are stored. The Communist spy flourishes in this clutter. Bigness makes subversion hard to detect, and it creates the need for more security officers, more civic restrictions, increased taxes, and a loss of public faith in governmental process. The population explosion has made the age a spy's paradise.

The scientist stands at the center of this breakdown. When he goes wrong politically, which he is more likely to do than most other men, he poses a great public threat. More knowledgeable and intelligent than the Nazi roughneck, he also has the technical materials to go wrong on a much larger scale. What worries Rebecca West mainly is the scientist's view of himself. His knowledge that society has come to rely increasingly on him has bloated his self-image to the point where he claims social omniscience. Pampered and highly paid, he readily supposes that his technical skill brings universal wisdom. Rebecca West dissents hotly from this opinion, arguing that technical training and moral insight are not the same thing. The claim that nuclear policy be left to the scientists and the corresponding claim that scientific knowledge be equally disseminated reflect the muddiest political thinking. Instead of exalting him as a seer, Rebecca West feels that the scientist has a much weaker claim to social omniscience than the nonscientist. His long technical training weighs against the development of nontechnical abilities, and his narrow vocational scope leaves him politically naïve. But he is more of a threat than the cyclamen grower of Nuremberg because his claim of moral superiority, unsupported by worldly experience, provides the basic stuff that Communist agents love to work with.

Science defines the cold-war traitor. Whereas the Nazi felt entitled to political power on the basis of his superior muscle-power, the Communist arrogates power to himself on the basis of his superior technical knowledge. Dr. Alan Nunn May, Lecturer of Physics at the University of London, had none of the crusading zeal of his earlier incarnation, William Joyce. Nunn May, who was tried and convicted in 1946, used his job in the atomic energy section of the National Research Council to collect information for Russia. Klaus Emil Fuchs, the head of the theoretical physics division of the atomic energy establishment at Harwell, is another scientist-spy who gave England's defense secrets to the Kremlin and thereby violated the Official Secrets Act. Rebecca West calls his arrest in 1950 "a new page . . . turned in the book of history." [41] His defense testimony revealed a starry-eyed altruism equivalent to a savior's complex:

> He had decided that the Western World was unfit to survive and betrayed it to the Soviet government; but the Soviet government also was not worthy, he would have to correct it in its turn. Here we are back in the religious zone again.

We do not stay in the religious zone very long. Fuchs's later actions disclose him as anything but starry-eyed or altruist: "he was a good party underground worker who knew all the tricks." [42] Inadequately screened by British Intelligence before given access to atomic research installations in the United States, this Communist of many years' standing did Russia the excellent service of discrediting British security.

Bruno Pontecorvo was another devout Communist who knew that propaganda and espionage have many uses. "Attractive and exuberant," and possessed of "great gifts," [43] Pontecorvo was given top security clearance and promoted to senior scientific officer at Harwell. Five screenings failed to detect his Communist ties. Ironically, he fomented distrust and disunity within the West without surrendering a shred of classified data. Ordered by his paymasters to go to Russia, he staged his leave-taking from England to attract as much public notice as possible. His ploy carried the day. Again, the ineptness of British security was made public knowledge; again, public confidence in British security was severely undermined.[44] A variation of this theme was played in 1951 by Donald Maclean, Guy Burgess, and Harold "Kim" Philby. Although none of the three men was a scientist, all were Communist agents who had infiltrated the executive branch of the British foreign service. Informed by Philby, the mysterious "third man," that they were about to be arrested, Burgess and Maclean fled England—again, as conspicuously as possible. Their "paperchase," [45] or carefully staged flight, stirred even more public indignation against British Intelligence than Pontecorvo's. Not only were the two Communists allowed to leave the country while at large; of particular embarrassment to Whitehall was the publication of the facts that Maclean had been arrested earlier for drunkenness and street brawling and that Burgess had a police record of homosexuality, drunken driving, illegal entry, and assault and battery. That these two Communist spies had been screened and checked by security officers raised universal doubt in the British government's ability to protect its citizens.

The last two spies Rebecca West studies were both more gifted and more highly trained than Burgess and Maclean. Stephen Ward and the man known only as "Colonel Abel" make William Joyce look like a simpleton. The subject of James B. Donovan's *Strangers on a Bridge: The Case of Colonel Abel* was probably the most powerful Russian spy in the western hemisphere at the time of his capture in 1957. And he earned his high post through his outstanding skill and versatility. It is impossible not to admire his brilliant accomplishments:

> He was remarkably talented. He could pass as a painter because he could, in fact, paint. . . . He was a fine linguist. . . . He was a skilled photographer, and he could do running repairs to any ordinary type of electrical equipment, even to elevators; and he was proficient both in carpentry and in the jeweller's craft to a degree which impressed those who did such work for a living. His musical knowledge was sufficient . . . to the extent of playing Bach and Villa-Lobos; and he was well enough acquainted with the sciences to regard books on mathematics and physics as light reading—not very advanced books, but not very easy ones either.[46]

Colonel Abel stands at the peak of contemporary espionage: not a grain of political idealism tinged his choice of a profession. Never a Marxist or a member of the Communist party, he was a professional spy who viewed his work as calmly as other men view theirs. Like any good professional, he brought a strong measure of skill and pride to his craft. If a capacity for lies and a contempt for personal welfare would help him do his job better, he would develop these traits without a drop of remorse.

Colonel Abel's counterpart, Stephen Ward, was another scientist who withdrew emotionally and morally from the things most of us live by. There can be doubt of his mastery as an osteopath, a bridge player, and a portrait painter: "He was a born professional: he was capable of acquiring all the skills necessary to the successful pursuit of an exacting occupation, and using them continuously at a high level." [47] Offsetting these skills was an obscure psychological quirk. Ward's favorite pastime was pimping, and he enjoyed practicing it in a way that undermined national security. Although not technically a traitor or a spy, he downgraded British security as thoroughly as any Soviet agent could wish in his wildest fantasies. He began making trouble by introducing Christine Keeler to both John Profumo, Minister of War, and Captain Eugene Ivanov, a naval attaché at the Russian embassy in London. As the mistress of a Soviet embassy official, Miss Keeler never had to mention the topic of classified information with Profumo to discredit British security. Her sexual association with him sufficed to do that.

Ward is a prime example of the specialist who responds thickly to everything outside his specialty. Duped by the Kremlin to wreck American confidence in the British government, he is a moral defective. Like most of his fellow spies, he embodies a truth first noticed by Rebecca West in her 1933 essay on Mrs. Pankhurst: that, beginning around 1900, unexceptional people have become the most powerful. The political leader of our century is rarely heroic. No aristocracy of talent directs the affairs of modern society; our kings and usurpers are either mediocrities or groundlings. Speaking of the Sarajevo attentat in *Black Lamb and Grey Falcon*, Rebecca West contrasts the stuffed Archduke Ferdinand and his frail, underfed killer, Princip, with the robust, well-made Bosnians lining the street. Of the mousy, eccentric William Joyce, she says, "There was nobody in the court who did not look superior to him." Of Dr. Alan Nunn May, "If ever Russia drops an atom bomb on Great Britain or America, the blame . . . must surely rest in part on this gifted and frivolous man." Of the small, weedy Klaus Emil Fuchs, "Fuchs . . . brought down on the unhappy world . . . the dreariness of the cold war." The information given to the Russians by the alcoholic wife-beater Maclean turned the Korean War in the North Koreans' favor.[48]

How does one explain the power of these mediocrities and defectives to inflict death upon large numbers of people? Rebecca West forces no single answer. Her attitude on the subject is best understood by repeating a remark she made in 1947 about the general deintellectualization of life since 1914.[49] This trend away from intellectual values and activities has split society. In the practical sphere of a scientific bureaucracy, it has created a hierarchy as well as a split. Denied power and position, William Joyce set out to build a society that would appreciate him. The same conviction of injured merit drove William Martin Marshall and William Vassall to steal classified materials. Government no longer stirs deep loyalties. The public cause, the public leader, and the public institution have become objects of distrust or attack. If government relied more on the creative energies of different kinds of people, not just scientists, the prevailing animus against political process might soften.

Too good-natured an acceptance of the political order, though, can harm. Sometimes complicity can be worse than treason. Margret Boveri begins her book, *Treason in the Twentieth Century*, by noting the benefits of treason to government:

> Treachery is a breach of trust. All human social life . . . rests on the assumption of the trustworthiness of the next man. At the same time, however, treason is a necessary historic development of politically organized societies. All radical political changes begin with treason.[50]

For society to move ahead, everybody must be tinged with treason: a nation's laws will stagnate unless challenged: opposition is essential to social well-being,. But government does more to encourage treason than simply to make dissent easy. Restricted information is so valuable that nations make treason highly attractive to foreign nationals holding security posts. This truth applies particularly to scientists, since it is so much more expedient to steal a scientific plan than to research and invent one. Yet, in the last analysis, espionage is bad economics. Aside from the time, energy, and money it takes, it rubs the grain of public faith. The usefulness of spies drives governments to hire more and more of them. The upshot is a governmental alarmism that mangles civil freedom: infiltration of security provokes counter-infiltration, double-agency, and a tightening of one's security arrangements.

This last policy creates the most ill will between a nation and its citizens. A nation must occasionally infringe upon civil liberties if it is to protect itself against spies. Yet the citizens being protected are likely to complain. Unfortunately, security often demands that intelligence officers work in secret. This necessity creates a political dilemma. Security cannot do its job if it explains its purposes to the public; at the same time, citizens of an open society are entitled to an explanation when their government curtails their freedom and raises their taxes. Democracy entails the free discussion fatal to undercover work. For this reason, a closed society can do its spying more efficiently. And there is nothing that the western countries can do to offset the handicap. The theory and the practice of spying will always clash in a democracy. If democratic institutions and laws are worth saving, it is because they take the added trouble of implementing themselves in public:

> A government often cannot, for security reasons, explain why it wishes to recover an agent. The Soviet people would not expect to be told, but a Western people would demand an explanation, and public confidence would be shaken if it were not forthcoming.

Rebecca West's commitment to the perfectibility of democracy is but one sign of her humanity. Flooding *The New Meaning of Treason* is a compassion that stems from her vast learning. Her ripe wisdom backs the claim, made in "The Strange Necessity," that the artist needs great stores of information. Sensitive to democratic procedures, she is capable of censuring her fellow adherants when they act badly: "In one libel action, Sir Oswald Mosley [leader of the British Union of Fascists in the 1930s] won, *and rightly won,* a verdict entitling him to £5000 in damages, and his costs." [51] (Italics mine.) Nor does she neglect Joyce's witty amiability, his brilliance as an organizer and a teacher, and his manly refusal to perjure himself in the dock. Yet she never forgets her theme. In spite of his merits, Joyce is not to be admired. Later, she insists just as hotly that spying and security must be removed from party politics; all governmental agencies must league together to prevent breaches in national security. This plea for legislative cooperation is her most important recommendation in *The New Meaning of Treason.* Once government takes security from the arena of partisan dispute, it recovers a sense of national wholeness. By narrowing the rifts between parties, between official agencies, and between scientist and nonscientist, a nation both blocks opportunities for spying and removes some of treason's chief motives.

This appeal brings to the fore Rebecca West's good sense, bracing analytical power, and moral passion. Much of *The New Meaning of Treason,* though, is not so persuasively argued. Like Dr. Johnson, she fiercely defends what she loves, and she is just as capable as he of beating her opponent with a club in order to win her argument. The suspension of consecutive logic, though dictated by a fine, deep-seated loyalty, creates awkward moments. For instance, Rebecca West implies that Joyce renewed his passport two months before its expiration in the summer of 1938 because he had foreknowledge of the Munich appeasement that was to take place that October. The implication carries no force; it rests uneasily on the assumption that Joyce knew German *and* British foreign policy, both before and after Chamberlain's flight. Her attacks on Communist traitors sometimes violate logic even more grossly. Kenneth Tynan, in fact, has accused her of supporting the anti-Communist browbeating of innocent people in the United States State Department.[52] To some extent, the accusation is just. It is disconcerting to hear her talk about "a generation conditioned to grumble at authority." Even more regrettable are some of her observations of political dissenters. She says of Morris Cohen (alias Peter John Kroger): "He had a comfortable enough

youth." Accordingly, Julius Rosenberg is said to have enjoyed "a pleasant enough existence" after leaving college, to
have worked "at reasonable salaries," and to have lived "in
an agreeable housing development." [53] Remarks like these
ignore the psychology of treason. They are the sort of thing
we say about others but never about ourselves. We see
ourselves as exceptional, precious, unique. That our salaries
are "reasonable" or our dwellings "agreeable" does not
soothe the dreamer and warrior in us.

The subject Rebecca West cannot discuss reasonably is
that of homosexuality. As in her other writings, homosexuality in *The New Meaning of Treason* bespeaks moral deg-
radation. A homosexual never does anything right; conversely, wrongdoers are often presented as effeminate.
William Vassall, the British embassy official who turned
over confidential papers to Russian agents, receives the full
blast of Rebecca West's antihomosexual bias. After touching
upon Vassall's skill as a photographer, his devotion as a son,
and his eagerness to perform kind deeds, she mentions his
homosexuality thus: "most important of all, he was a homosexual." Why is this feature of Vassall's personality "most
important of all"? Is it such a moral blemish that it cancels
his merits? Once on the topic of Vassall's homosexuality,
Rebecca West is transfixed. She suggests, without a scrap
of supporting evidence, that a Communist homosexual
lover took Vassall from London to Moscow: "It is . . .
very easy to imagine him feeling mild enthusiasm for communism combined with an ardent passion for a Communist.
There is no evidence of this, but it could have happened." [54]
Later, she protests that Vassall was allowed to continue
spying for the Russians after his chiefs at Naval Intelligence
had found him out. There is no reason for the protest. If
Vassall's superiors did not stop him, they were probably
supplying him with false documents in order to mislead
the Russians; the Admiralty would not give up an advantage
like this hastily. And if there is some other explanation, it is
difficult to see why the Admiralty should feel obliged to
share it with Rebecca West.

Flaws like these mar *The New Meaning of Treason*. In

her conclusion, which is also marred, she says that none of the spies whose cases she reviewed betrayed their country for material gain. The demogogue Joyce, the cool professional Colonel Abel, the homosexual Vassall, and the pimp Ward all acted treacherously out of a common passion for disorder and excitement. This passion, she continues, is a public threat because it strikes such a responsive chord with the death-drift in us all. Her argument is valid, but inconclusive. Yes, we all have a nihilistic streak which delights in lawbreaking. Yet the streak may be something other than an appetite for death. In the cases of Joyce, Morris Cohen, and Julius Rosenberg, anyway, it may have been a case of injured merit. Perhaps we sometimes sympathize with convicted felons and take joy when lawbreakers escape because we cannot strike back in any other way at the society that has tamed our blood and looked askance at our gifts.

But why should these resentments flare out during the postwar period? The military actions at Korea, Suez, and Vietnam have been among the most unpopular on record. Democracy, or what nowadays passes for democracy, has created vacuums and gaps into which interference has been rushing from both right and left. This dissent cannot be explained by fixing the label of grumbler upon a generation of people. *The New Meaning of Treason* fails as political prophecy. Yet it is nourished by love of country; by firsthand experience in the courtrooms and streets of bomb-gutted cities; and by the knowledge that the law must always rebuild itself in the light of social change. We should not only be grateful for this fully committed wisdom. We should also use it as the groundwork of our programs and policies as we chart our political future.

4

The Comet

Rebecca West published *The Fountain Overflows* at age sixty-four and *The Birds Fall Down* at age seventy-four. These late novels surpass overwhelmingly the four that came out between 1918 and 1936. In *The Summing Up*, W. Somerset Maugham spoke of "the intimacy, the broad human touch and the animal serenity which the greatest writers alone can give." [1] Rebecca West approaches Maugham's literary ideal in her late fiction. By setting her novels in the Edwardian era, she wrote about things she lived with for many years. By waiting twenty years between her fourth and fifth novels, she developed the artistry to do justice to this wealth of knowledge. Her court-reporting trained her eye and also taught her clarity and directness of expression.

The Court and the Castle mentions Fielding's preference of observation over "a creative faculty" in a novelist. [2] Rebecca West's two late novels take their cue from Fielding in that they are more retrospective than inventive. Their mastery stems largely from their knack of turning up and then exploiting the key detail. But the books have more in common than technique. Both center around a sensitive girl growing up in a deteriorating family. The malaise breaking down the two girls' families is also undermining western culture at large. *The Fountain Overflows* and *The Birds Fall Down* describe societies in decline. They also describe their author's complex attitude to the nineteenth century. Falling from imperial grandeur, these fast-changing societies are as resplendent as comets. But the brilliance is the work of breakdown and disintegration. Both books are laced with images of collapse, noncommunication, and incoherence; both, finally, turn on the irony of a female growing up in a crumbling male world.

What sets the two late novels off from all Rebecca West's other work—not only her earlier fiction—is their carefully ordered style. Although it is hard to think of her prose rolling off anybody's pen, she once claimed that she writes very quickly.[3] If anywhere, this haste makes itself felt phonetically. Rebecca West has always tended to wordiness, a serious handicap to a writer whose style is basically periodic to begin with. Occasionally, her ear deserts her, as it does in the following quotation from *Black Lamb and Grey Falcon*, where sentence movement runs afoul of a jawbreaking cluster of Latinisms: "The French . . . were able to demand a *quid pro quo* for erecting the scaffolding of obfuscation that surrounded the trial." Other sentences in the same book are weighted down by a chain of abstract nouns: "The infringement here was of an unpublished dynastic regulation instead of the published law." Elsewhere, inattention to verbal rhythms produces lopsided syntax: "They really cannot conceive of a centralized government at all as otherwise than an evil." (The same idea could be stated more smoothly thus: "They can only conceive of a centralized government as evil.") Nor is this bloated style confined to *Black Lamb and Grey Falcon*. In *The New Meaning of Treason*, we are told that Bruno Pontecorvo's presence in the USSR in 1955 was "definitely ascertained." And *A Train of Powder* gives this description of Hamburg in 1949: "But if one stopped in the right street one could refresh oneself at a large tea shop, which was full of people, mostly women, and all Germans." [4] (None of the sentence's meaning would be lost if the sentence were rewritten thus: "In the right street you could refresh yourself at a large tea shop, full of Germans, mostly women.") An addiction to link verbs often robs Rebecca West's sentences of pep and economy. A writer given to a latinate vocabulary and syntax should use transitive verbs in the active voice whenever possible, especially in main clauses of long sentences. But her work before 1956 cries for editing. Not only could the copula be cut from many of her sentences. The relative pronoun or subordinating conjunction introducing the copula could also go. These words are italicized in the following sentences:

> As we got nearer the town, we saw *that there were* people encamped on the brow of each hill.

> The party [Mosley's BUF] . . . made a practice of interrupting and breaking up *the* Communist meetings *which were being held* in London, especially the East End.[5]

The same proclivity for link verb prevents her from availing herself of the clarity and smoothness furnished by parallel construction: "One of his colleagues objected that there were no shops there and it was impossible that it could ever become a shopping centre." Rephrased thus the sentence is both shorter and better balanced: "One of his colleagues objected that there were no shops there and that it was impossible to imagine it a shopping centre." A similar benefit occurs by supplying a transitive verb and then omitting the comma and link-verb cluster from this sentence: "Some day some such incident might provoke the Russians to a sudden warlike act, and the Third World War would be upon us."[6] Here is the emended version: "Some day some such incident might provoke the Russians to a sudden warlike act and bring the Third World War upon us." The relative-copula combination, the "There is here" cluster at the beginning of sentences, and the practice of starting consecutive sentences or independent clauses with "but" still survive in the late fiction. But mostly she only adds words to give a sentence a better balance. Her later style has spine and sinew: the sentences are usually shorter than those in the earlier books, the word order is more regular and rhythmic, the figures of speech more natural. Style subserves theme; for Rebecca West's command of her subjects is so sure-handed that she has no need to substitute verbal acrobatics for a well-executed plot and story line.

Full of warmth and ripeness, *The Fountain Overflows* probably reveals more of Rebecca West than any of her other books. On this score, it roughly parallels *The Court and the Castle.* But the novel's intimacy surpasses that of the earlier book by virtue of its more personal subject matter. Instead of dealing with ideas, *The Fountain Overflows* shows what Rebecca West was like before she began to think abstractly. It takes us back to her childhood, recreating the complex mood of music, politics, and financial worries that marked these years. What moves the reader here is the vivid sense of family life. Rebecca West conveys through tone and incident the sensation of growing up in a family like that of her parents. Like the narrator's mother, hers was a musician of Scottish background; like Piers Aubrey, her father was an editor, a widely traveled war correspondent, and a disciple of Herbert Spencer.[7] These biographical tie-ins both deepen and sharpen the novel's feminist theme, hinted at in the epigraph: "The cistern contains: the fountain overflows." Harvey Curtis Webster, in *Saturday Review*, reads the epigraph, from Blake, as a dualistic value judgment: fountains that overflow are better than cisterns that merely contain.[8] Webster's reading, though basically correct, says nothing about symbolism. The upward-gushing fountain, for instance, may be phallic, i.e., the jet of water that wastefully overflows its container. But the fountain can also be female; in this case, it represents the fully outgoing love whose overflowing abundance refreshes everything it touches while constantly renewing itself. But as this soaring love reaffirms itself, it also overflows with cares and worries. Women are asked to do too much. If too many people dip their cups into the fountain, the fountain may tip, go dry, or overflow. Whereas the dashing Piers Aubrey does as he pleases, his wife sacrifices her good looks and a concert career to raise her family. These meanings and more rise from the epigraph. Rebecca West dedicated the book to her sister and may have played on the word "cistern" to contrast mother-love and sister-love. (Rose Aubrey, the narrator, has two sisters.) On the other hand, the water tilting steadily into a fountain spells out the loss and waste that go with any burst of vitality. The water stored in a cistern is liable to stagnate, but the sparkling water that dances over the brim of a fountain dances with life.

The Fountain Overflows generates more bounce than any

of Rebecca West's other fictions. Elizabeth Janeway praised the book's lavish movement and richness of event in the *New York Times Book Review*:

> It is very like Dickens. It is as full of characters—odd and even, but mostly odd—as a pudding of plums; full of incident, full of family delights, full of parties and partings, strange bits of London, the lobby of the House of Commons, a classic murder with portraits of the murderer, the murderee and a couple of innocent bystanders, bill collectors, kitchen fires, good food, and a considerable number of ghosts. . . . In short, this is a very novelish sort of novel, old-fashioned, busy and extremely readable.[9]

The opening pages ironically fix movement as the stable condition of the Aubrey family's life. The family is making ready to move from Edinburgh to Lovegrove, a seedy London suburb where Piers Aubrey has found a job editing a small newspaper. Cordelia, the eldest child, the twins Mary and Rose, and the baby Richard Quin were all born in South Africa and have already lived in Capetown and Durban before coming to Edinburgh. This unsettled life has denied the Aubreys the processes of friendship and interchange between a person and his environment. The coming move to London, although they do not know it, is to rain upon them still more insecurity and clutter. Ironically, just prior to setting out for the instability of big city life in chapter one, the Aubrey children visit a stable. The incident charts the way for what is to happen to them later. The horses they see are "kind creatures."[10] But the same kind creatures that let mice share their stalls stamp so furiously at night that they frighten the children. Here is an emblem of the complexity of life. Life is uncertain and knotty because nothing has only one meaning: acts of kindness can inflict pain, telling a lie can be kinder than telling the truth, and what seems generosity can also be construed as selfishness.

The Fountain Overflows is a celebration, a criticism, and a self-exploration. As has been mentioned, the ordeal of the Aubrey children is that they must grow up in a climate of incoherence and breakdown. Rebecca West uses the city to convey the sickness of modern life. The larger the city, the more pervasive the sickness. Note the loss that goes with the Aubreys' move to London from Edinburgh, where moral and educational standards are high and where Clare Aubrey, the mother, knows many people. The Aubreys are strangers in the hurly-burly of London. Aubrey's new employer refuses to meet Aubrey personally. When people do meet in London, it is usually at odd times and in odd places. But what amazes is that they meet at all. The British home secretary is called a minotaur.[11] Modern life is a maze; everybody is lost, and nobody has reason to hope he will someday find himself. Ruled out as a guide from the start is leadership—either in business or in government. As he was in A *Train of Powder* and *The New Meaning of Treason*, the modern leader is unfit. The mayor of Lovegrove, whose wife becomes inflamed by another man, is "a short, stout man. . . . His eyes were bleared and his cheeks puffy." [12] Oswald Pennington is a stockish MP, less familiar with civil law than most private citizens, let alone public servants. Harry Phillips, head of the only family the Aubreys get to know in London, owns a gleaming roadster and a membership in the local Conservative Club but lacks the respect of his wife and daughter.

Soon after their arrival in London, the Aubreys feel this division. They are cut off from everyone they meet. Because they are poor in a money-dominated society, they do not count socially. Because their cultural superiority has not lifted them from the slum, they are despised by their neighbors and schoolmates. Aubrey is a genius but is usually out of pocket and out of a job. Whereas British politics are run by minotaurs and mediocrities, Piers Aubrey has hardly any public identity. Here is Aubrey's self-commentary:

> I have no party. Only a handful of men in all of England believe what I believe. Many people read me, and seem to think well of my writings. But almost nobody credits a word I say. It is a very curious feeling. . . . I exist and I do not exist.[13]

The Aubreys reflect their time. Their home mirrors the debasement of public taste, first, by cheap journalism and, next, by the "star" system in the entertainment industry.

Cordelia, ironically the most heartless Aubrey child, gains public favor as a violinist on the strength of her prettiness. The twins, Mary and Rose, put off *their* concert careers in order to acquire technique. But despite their superior attitude and aptitude, they are usually pitied for being less musical than Cordelia. And when not misunderstood by outsiders, the Aubreys always misread each other. As did *The Thinking Reed*, *The Fountain Overflows* insists on the opaqueness of persons: there is no dynamic lifeline between people, and the most total strangers are the people we live with.

The family, then, cannot fend off the furious pace of modern life. The novel's symbol for the speed, the disconnectedness, and the machine mentality of our century is the automobile. Owned by the rich cockney Harry Phillips but driven by his chauffeur, science's latest glory only runs well when its owner is not at the wheel. (Phillips always breaks something whenever he tries to drive the car.) Rose's elation over riding in a car for the first time is stifled by the uncomfortable knowledge that no horse is pulling the car forward. The horse, with its strength, beauty, and awesomeness, represents generally the male principle and more specifically the father. The leaderless car, which breaks down at its master's touch, conveys both the disorder and the deenergization of a science-centered world. Change and incoherence are the only fixed points in early-century London. Like love, reason cannot halt the trend. Aubrey's marginal public status and Cordelia's public acclaim attest to the unreason that moves public choice. And, as she usually does, Rebecca West tightens her novel by carrying this social principle inside the Aubrey home. One basic lesson in unreason Rose learns is that things have one meaning for grownups and another for children. And as she gets older, she sees unreason reaching beyond event into personality:

My father, though very cruel, was very kind.

He was often kind, but he was also ungrateful.[14]

By conceding that human truths often clash with reason, Rebecca West puts forward no do-as-you-please morality.

The things we hold closest do violate reason, but because they are sacred. Rose is too young to see the human logic in the following advice, given by her mother: "It is always disgraceful for you to tell a lie, but if other people tell lies there is often a very good reason for it, and you must just note that they are lying and pass on." [15] Clare Aubrey's advice extends the idea, stated in *The Court and the Castle*, that kings cannot act morally. To withhold harsh judgment in situations where a harsh judgment is called for can lead to moral anarchy. Yet treating people better than they deserve is the height of graciousness. Clare finds herself forced to choose between her husband and her children. Her choice reflects her belief that life is God's greatest gift and that we must defend it any way we can. Another character perjures herself for the sake of her sister. By not condemning her, Rebecca West endorses the human truth that duty to family overrides legal bounds. Like kings, we are condemned to do things which, done in a different context, would invite blame.

There is but little distance between man's failure to frame universally relevant laws and the bugbear of original sin. Nor does Rebecca West rule out an Augustinian reading of *The Fountain Overflows*. Brought home several times in the book is the idea that the people who inflict the most pain are the ones who act out of love. Other evidence supports the claim that Rebecca West finds action inherently corrupt. Cordelia and Rose are always put down when they attempt to take charge of a family problem. All conflicts do not dissolve in direct action, and the girls learn that, rather than speaking out, they must sometimes feign insensitivity and remain quiet in order to stay sane and civilized. If restraint seems to beat action as a solution to human problems, certain sorts of action cause more harm than others. The most lethal of these is the sort independently undertaken. The most objectionable characters in the book are the most individualistic. These shakers strew pain wherever they go because they violate process: no act can equal in importance the context in which it takes place. Rose says of her childhood, "Mary and Richard Quin and I were really not separate beings." [16] Elsewhere she speaks of the warmth and fun that came from physical contact with her brother and sister. But whereas the three Aubrey children liked to touch each other, Cordelia shied from physical expressions of love. It is never said outright that Cordelia's physical reserve accounted for her later nervousness. There *is* a causal chain, though, including her disapproval of her parents, her craving to leave home, and her concert career. By rebuffing her brother and sisters physically and her parents morally, she loses touch with the forces that shaped her life. Instead of being self-motivated, Cordelia forfeits selfhood. She is conventional in the most pejorative sense of the word. All her values are dictated by popular musical tastes. It is apposite that her heartless withdrawal from her family should end in a heart ailment. Her violin-playing denies life. The news of Harry Phillips's death reaches her at one of her concerts, and she tries to kill herself after hearing from a celebrated teacher that she has no musical skill.

Rebecca West, then, goes to a great deal of trouble to show her suspicion of human endeavor. Cordelia's actions beget only grief. Whatever life she retains after her suicide attempt has nothing to do with her exertions. But does Cordelia's example mean that all action must end in futility? Or can one avoid choosing between the rapid death of self-expression and the slow death of self-restraint? The best way both to regulate and to dignify our conduct is by using love as a measure. And since most of us learn love unconsciously as children in our parents' home, Rebecca West uses the family as a storage cell of heart-knowledge, cheer, and rootedness. The various circles and ovals in the book symbolize the closed arc, the overarching protectiveness, of family love.

But what is this family love like? Most of all it is an outgoing of the heart that, asking nothing for itself, frustrates harshness and promotes joy. Clare once says to Rose, "Have another raisin. If you roll the little withered ones between your fingers they taste sweet and rich like the big fat ones." [17] A warm, gentle touch, then, marks the difference between opposites. But the outgoing of love need not be physical. A gathering of four people who love each other rids a house of its poltergeist. When Clare sells some paintings, whose value she had kept secret from her husband, her buyer is an art dealer named Wertheimer—Clare's motherly protection of her children having ratified the worth of her home (German *heim*-home).

But by protecting her children, Clare chides herself for failing her husband. Her remorse bears out once again the Westian imperative that duty often makes nonsense of morals. But her remorse also explains the impurity of love. The Aubreys' marriage is a cat's cradle of betrayals and communication failures. Clare's keeping to herself the true worth of the portraits hanging in the children's room is matched by Aubrey's private knowledge of a hidden cabinet above the fireplace. Love, then, cannot be trusted. When it serves order and joy, it does so at a heavy price. At other times, it is either helpless or a force for evil. Clare's attitude toward love, stated in quotation below, is probably close to that of her author:

> This is the worst of life, that love does not give us common sense but is a sure way of losing it. We love people, and we say that we are going to do more for them than friendship, but it makes such fools of us that we do far less, indeed sometimes what we do could be mistaken for the work of hatred.[18]

As has been said, love does not solve the problems of the Aubreys and its failure weighs heavily. Even when love works for gain, it does so quietly. Rebecca West knows that love is neither measurable nor translatable into specific acts. She does make us wonder, though, if love, as man's greatest gift, cannot occur more forcefully and positively than through an act of moral delicacy. If love can cause so much wreckage, why does it not yield an equal intensity of joy? And why must it be accompanied by tact?

Rebecca West answers these questions dramatically. Whatever survives in the novel, like Cordelia's sanity and the moral balance of the other children, does so by the power of love. Rebecca West has not finished writing about the ironic subject of love. She comes back to it in *The Birds*

Fall Down. And according to a magazine interview, *The Fountain Overflows* is the first number of a projected trilogy, the next installment of which will pit the corrupting nature of power against the honorable nature of failure.[19] This tension dominated *Black Lamb and Grey Falcon*. The political and religious focus of that book suggests, along with Rebecca West's growing tendency to revisit the past, that she may unify the theme around the subject of love. Love can change failure into success, and renunciation can outstrip action if prompted by love.

The center of the community of loving in *The Fountain Overflows* is Clare Aubrey. Wife and mother, teacher and musician, Clare surpasses aesthetically the stylized, static Harriet Hume as Rebecca West's female ideal. Whereas Harriet lived alone, Clare manages a large family. And while Harriet changed nobody, Clare's influence on her children is monumental. She teaches them, first, that a quick imagination can offset material disadvantages. Although poor, her children cultivate musical technique and interpretive power, which in turn, nourish their faculties of restraint, balance, and compassion. Having played the piano and read Shakespeare from their earliest years, Mary and Rose discover that they have more, and not less, than children from other families, as they had first thought. Clare's example turns out to be a preparation for life as well as a grounding in skills. By calling Clare "the embodiment of integrity, both as artist and as woman," a *Saturday Review* reviewer acknowledges the outstanding service she does for her children. For a more extended summary of her character, let us go back to Elizabeth Janeway;

> Let us not call her a saint. . . . Clare Aubrey lives in the center of life, at full stretch. Inhuman demands are made on her. It is her salvation that she is always ready and almost always able to meet them. She gave up a career as a concert pianist to marry Piers Aubrey, and now she deals with the bill collectors, the friends who have become enemies, and the exigencies of ordinary daily living on not quite enough money. . . . Clare Aubrey is convincing

both as an artist . . . and as a person fatally in love who draws life instead of death from the wound.[20]

In giving up a concert career, she gave up much; according to her teacher, she played Schumann's *Carnaval* and Mozart's Concerto in C Minor "better than any other woman who had ever lived." Being a wife and becoming a mother also costs her her looks. Rose calls her "not good-looking," "beaky," and devoid of "feminine graces": "She was too thin, her nose and forehead were shiny like bone, and her features were disordered." [21] As she did in *The Judge*, Rebecca West conveys through Clare her belief that a woman's love and sacrifice are measured by grief: a woman's lot hardens in direct proportion to her devotion. The constant strain of dealing with cranks and creditors and of managing a home on short funds makes her ugliness a badge of honor. But the feminism of the book goes beyond Clare. Rosamund, her niece, turns the mind from music to statuary and a new kind of feminist ideal. As the rose of the world, she overcomes all handicaps; that any flower, let alone a fine rose, can flourish in a London slum is a miracle. As the point of union between the human and divine, the miraculous rose is fully perfected humanity. Rose says of her, "She was simply there." [22] Like a pillar, she is solid, whole, and capable of expressing intensity of being without speech or movement. She is first seen in a garden, playing by a rabbit hutch. The innocence and teeming life built into this first glimpse squares with her later choice of nursing as a career. She stands for life — its fullness, preservation, and renewability.

But Rosamund's characterization, if intellectually pleasing, is artistically ragged. Statuesque and slow moving, she comes close to immobility, and her excellence is nearly equated with blankness. By calling Rosamund "very contadictory," [23] Rebecca West is smuggling a detail into her book that does not belong. But perhaps this judgment is premature. The golden, honeyish Rosamund is slated to reappear in the projected sequel (entitled, before abandoned, "This Real Night") to *The Fountain Overflows* together with Richard Quin, the mercurial son of the Aubreys.[24] Rebecca West may well supply in that book a chain of events that makes good Rosamund's contradictory nature.

Rosamund and Clare form half of a familiar dualist equation. The harmony, rootedness, and solidity that define them differs in kind from the associations raised by the men in the book. Sharp steel instruments, the stamping hooves of horses, the banging of defective machinery, and pointed objects in general signal the male principle. The poker that breaks Rosamund's window, when her house is inhabited by a poltergeist, is maleness incarnate. As in Virginia Woolf's *To the Lighthouse,* Rebecca West uses the window to stand for interchange and perception. Clare likes to sit by windows; the careering poker, by breaking a window, offends against both personal communication and domestic calm. Elsewhere, the symbolism is more playful. Another phallic device, the flute belonging to Rosamund's death-driven father, raises comparisons with an enema-syringe.

Piers Aubrey recalls a Rebecca West character we hear about but never meet—Ellen Melville's father in *The Judge.* Both men are Irish, both marry exceptional women, both lose their money gambling on the stock exchange, and both desert their families. Aubrey also resembles characters outside Rebecca West's fiction. This brilliant polemicist, who once debated seven hours with Bernard Shaw and whose pamphlet on judicial reform is "as good as anything Swift ever wrote," [25] calls to mind the brilliant failures of C. P. Snow. Aubrey's psychological burden is his dedication to self-ruin. Love of failure prevents him from being the pillar, or pier, which upholds his family, and it also robs him of becoming an MP, or peer of the realm, a post he wanted "more than anything in the world." [26] He therefore takes jobs beneath his ability. But after he endows them with dignity and honor, his self-destructiveness bars him from sharing the rewards. "His lifelong wrestling match with money" typifies his tendency to rub raw this obscure nerve-ending:

> He was infatuated with it [i.e., money] though he could not get on good terms with it. He felt towards it as a man

of his type might have felt towards a gipsy mistress, he loved it and hated it, he wanted hugely to possess it and then drove it away, so that he nearly perished of his need for it.[27]

Aubrey's crusades for social justice chime with his passion for disgrace. So gorged is he with self-contempt that public crusading is the only constructive effort he is capable of. He is Rebecca West's fully developed public man, or lunatic. He embraces causes because he cannot bear the things closest him—his home, his family, himself. He is introduced discreetly in the first chapter, where he secretly sells the family's furniture for a small fraction of its value and then goes on to gamble the money away. Before he leaves home, he gives two bravura performances, one spoken and one written, both in the political sphere, and neither fully perceived by the reader. One day Rose goes with him to the House of Commons, where, by dint of dazzling verbal swordplay, he blackmails the MP, Sir Oswald Pennington, into working to establish an appellate court. It is proper that this performance should take place in Parliament, the fulcrum of masculinist Britain in its imperial decline. Also proper is the fact that soon after his interview with Pennington, that is, when Rose is proudest of him, he leaves his family forever. Aubrey's self-scorn would never have let him enjoy both public and private esteem. His second bravura piece, a prophetic look at twentieth-century politics, is briefly summarized after he decamps. He foresees government by the mediocre giving way to dictatorships, large-scale wars, and the aerial destruction of cities. The forecast hurls Aubrey into despair. He predicts the filth and madness of our century because the same forces throb inside him. After writing his pamphlet, he acts like a man returned from the dead. He leaves the house the same way he had entered it, alone and by stealth.

Mentioned in *The New Meaning of Treason* is the frequent occurrence of exceptional men who lose everything by demanding too much of themselves: "Those who foresee the future and recognize it as tragic are often seized by a madness which forces them to commit the very acts which makes it certain that what they dread shall happen." [28] Ironically, the fortunes of the family rise after Aubrey leaves. Friends help Clare and the children; Cordelia gives up her degrading career; Mary and Rose launch their promising careers; Clare brings money into the home by selling her original Gainsborough and Lawrence portraits. The argument thus moves to the mythical sphere. Aubrey is the tragic scapegoat-mad poet who must be driven out before a sane, orderly routine can come to life.

The mythical argument is carried forward by Jock, Clare's cousin and Rosamund's flute-playing father. He, too, sets aside an extraordinary intellect, surrenders to chance, and winds up cursing the light. Whereas Aubrey has shifted his loyalties from the home to politics, Jock goes a step farther. Although he earns a fine salary, he spends it all on psychical research. The threat he embodies is more basic than that of Aubrey. Like Aubrey, he is often likened to darkness, the totem for evil in Manichean dualism. But his tall, stringy frame, his similarity to a snake,[29] and his Scots ancestry summon the devil, or Old Nick, who often materializes as a Scot. As a flautist, he is a reverse Oedipus, leading his wife and daughter into the hell of poverty, shame, and occultism. Rebecca West wants us to censure Jock's interest in the occult. Any chipping away at the wall separating the present and the future disrupts the normal rhythms of life. Her 1952 statement, "I do not even find in myself any great curiosity as to whether my soul is immortal or not," [30] expresses her faith in orderly process. To accept the natural order, one must also accept doubt. The day Rose's pride betrays her into reading minds is the same day her brother gets seriously sick.

The day also marks the first visit of a Phillips to the Aubrey home. The relationship between the two families typifies the discreet beauty of *The Fountain Overflows*. Although the Phillipses come to the Aubreys by way of "one of the most notorious murder cases of the Edwardian era," [31] Rebecca West underplays the public side of the case—the murder, the police investigation, and the legal give-and-take of the trial. What she stresses instead is the effect of the murder on the Aubrey home. The Aubreys are touched in several places by the crime. That Nancy Phillips and her aunt should choose to stay with the Aubreys, whom they only met two days before, comments starkly on the impersonality of modern city life. And more than impersonality comes into play in the fact that Queenie Phillips killed her husband to run away with a clerk from the real-estate firm that owns the Aubrey's home.

But these events are largely secondary. The value of the novel dwells, not in story or event, but in bodily warmth. The novel takes us into a child's world, where the wonder and pain of growing up have a life of their own. We see what it is like to be a child rebuffed by a preoccupied parent. But we see, too, that children have their own defenses and weapons. The tensions both between and within generations take shape differently. Rebecca West devotes little more than one chapter to the Phillips ordeal. Cordelia's violin-playing, on the other hand, spills over into several chapters. Certain cherished events, like the annual family Christmas, have a recurring magic. Rebecca West also introduces dreams, family myths, and made-up animals. The early chapters, where the children are small, oscillate between actual and imagined events, proving that, to a child and to the grown-up who never drives out the child, some events are no less real for never having happened.

So personal a novel risks curdling into overstatement, sentimentality, and preachiness. By adopting the first-person narrative, Rebecca West offsets the risk. Often Rose will stand back from her earlier self to make a moral point: "My mother sighed with impatience at what was not to sound a reasonable remark until half a century had passed." At other times, the young girl experiencing an event gives way to the mature narrator for the purpose of framing the event within its social context: "Though we had little money we had a servant, in those days even poor households had servants": "This was an astonishing pronouncement in those days, when dietetic error flourished." Another device which both dispels wistfulness and deepens the book's historical thrust is the mention of something that happened at a time be-

tween the events taking place in the book and the writing
about those events: "I cannot . . . cancel my intention of
living there some day, though it was destroyed by a bomb in
the Second World War." [32] By taking advantage of the self-
irony and of the time-sweep afforded by the first-person narrative, Rebecca West develops Rose's character in depth,
showing us Rose both as a child and as an adult.

Rose's shifting vantage point is just one way the novel refreshes itself. The treatises on musical technique and theory,
pleasingly varied and well spaced, help flesh out the domestic
routine of the Aubreys. London comes to live in the same
way—through descriptions in different keys of its parks,
buildings, and train stations. Events like the Boer War, scientific advances like the car, and the new barbarism of the
Phillips family certify London as the hub of a fast-changing
society. Within the Aubrey home, though, the passing of
time is less well certified. The children acquire new skills and
new interests, but unlike the Baines girls in Bennett's *The
Old Wives' Tale*, they develop only superficially. Their personalities take shape by fiat rather than by event, the children rarely doing things in succeeding chapters beyond their
powers in earlier ones.

But this blemish is offset by the masterstroke of compres-
sion that ends the novel. The last scene, cinching together
the realities of sex, money, and a career in music, carries Rose
and Mary into adult life. They have just given a private re-
cital of some songs written by a young composer. The moment is one of surpassing achievement: the girls have earned
their first money as concert pianists, and they have also just
discovered that they have both won musical scholarships.
Avoiding a pat climax of event, Rebecca West uses the twin
blessing as an occasion for pain, growth, and recognition.
That the girls learn of their awards away from their mother
mutes some of the glory. Rose is further shaken by the
young composer whose songs she has just played: "What was
music? I suddenly felt sick because I did not know the answer." Perhaps every decisive step forward provokes a back-
ward look. Rose's fear and unreadiness betoken real growth.
Having arrived both as a person and as a musician in the
novel's last paragraph, she looks into the "dark, kind, smiling

Eastern face" of her host and is then "swept on by the strong flood of which [she is] a part." [33] Rose welcomes the rush of new life because life is the only choice for the living. Affirmed together with her healthy organic growth is a context for her nature. The host's "dark" complexion merges nicely with the Manichean dualism used generally in the book to symbolize evil and good. His "Eastern" look, when joined to the fact that he owns a private ballroom, suggests the rising social power of Jews in London. By noting his "kind, smiling" expression, Rose may well be describing both her liking for her host and her cheerful acceptance of the change ("the strong flood") he represents. This final look east, i.e., toward the source of energy and light, confirms Rose's emergence. It also confirms Rebecca West as the writer of a major novel.

The Birds Fall Down proves that Rebecca West is still a developing artist. If *The Fountain Overflows* recalled Dickens, the craft of the later book turns the mind to Conrad. The volley of events, the cozy, crackling make-believe world of children, and the use of the home as a community of loving give way in *The Birds Fall Down* to drafty train stations, hotel rooms in strange cities, and family disunity. The Rowan family is divided. Two sons never even get into the novel, and the parents stop living together after the first chapter. Their daughter Laura notes the blasted state of the marriage at this point: "It was not that her father and mother were quarrelling. They could not have done that, her father was not even there to be quarrelled with." [34] Rebecca West's darkening moral vision, like her growing concern with remoteness and impersonality as symptoms of modern life, goes back to *The Thinking Reed*. The reconciliation of Isabelle and Marc Sallafranque expresses a faith in the power of sexual love that waned in the next twenty years; for sexuality in the two late novels ends in adultery, desertion, and murder.

Like Anthony Burgess's *Tremor of Intent* and Kingsley Amis's *The Anti-Death League*, which came out the same year as *The Birds Fall Down*, Rebecca West's latest work uses the form of the thriller to make a serious moral statement. But the work stands closer to Conrad's *The Secret Agent,* than it does to its 1966 counterparts. It follows Conrad's practice of building suspense and then destroying it in order to change our thinking about the way people react to stress. So when Rebecca West allows several hours and a police investigation to come between a murder and her account of it, she is trying to catch something both basic and unrevealed in life. The slapstick, the melodrama, and the craving for sleep during stress brings the novel closer to the events it describes. *The Birds Fall Down* is Rebecca West's boldest fiction. Saturated in the Hegelian thought that dominated Europe for nearly a century, it expresses a vision, frames the vision both historically and philosophically, and criticizes it from a modern standpoint. Although the book does not challenge like much of Conrad and Joyce, it tries new things with fictional technique. Rebecca West goes beyond stream of consciousness by showing the brokenness of nonmental events ranging from private conversation to public affairs. In short, she presents the discontinuity of the mind as a social fact. What emerges most forcibly from *The Birds Fall Down* is the wall between people. In *The Fountain Overflows,* everybody in the Aubrey home was a stranger to everybody else. In the later book, people can refer to the same thing with the same word yet intend different meanings.

A world in which strangers prove more friendly than close relatives is bound to terrify. This terror is all the more profound for being so hideously beautiful: "The world was . . . coloured and intricate like jewellery, but horrible." [35] Rebecca West's imagination grows wilder and more scenic with the years. Rather than discussing the Rowans's marriage, she mentions in the novel's second paragraph that the English accent of Edward Rowan's Russian wife has deteriorated. Later, Tania's grief at seeing her mother shrunken and torn by illness translates itself into a hysterical act. Rebecca West drives home Tania's hysteria with a macabre analogy:

"Mother!" said Tania in a whisper. "Mother!" She caught her hat to her bosom and drove her hatpin through the bird which trimmed it, as if she were killing something which must not be permitted to exist for one more moment.[36]

The macabre, the unexpected, and the outrageous hold sway. The novel's methodology suggests that Rebecca West planned *The Birds Fall Down*, like Euripedes' *The Bacchae*, as a paean to madness as the prime mover of the world. Her description of a Paris street murder mixes buffoonery and bloodshed. She gains a jarring comic horror by avoiding the murder until she has logged in the reactions of the passersby. The bizarre happenings, the impressionistic technique, and the far-reaching political implications come straight from Conrad. (In a 1960 lecture, she spoke of Conrad's political thought as "full of . . . wisdom, strangely applicable to our day.") First, "a tall blonde woman . . . fell back into the arms of a bearded young man in a frock coat and striped trousers." The image of the young man catching the woman shows how quickly people can appear ludicrous: "As he caught her his monocle flew out of his eye and swung off in a circle on its black ribbon, at the same time that his top-hat slid off the back of his head." The irony thickens as the policeman who comes to restore order misplaces his whistle and breaks the strap on his truncheon: "All his movements were going wrong, as if he were an actor in a harlequinade." [37] Later, when the author reports the hiding of the murder weapon, she uses a slow-motion technique, describing in close detail the steps by which the weapon is wrapped, tied, and finally stowed away. This ironical handling of event not only involves the reader more actively. It tends to deny the age tragic grandeur; the undercutting of heroism and suspense gives the sense that nothing these characters do can matter.

The idea of a stricken humanity caught in a stricken, down-coursing society occurs in both the novel's title and epigraph.

The last line of the passage from Conway Power's "Guide to a Disturbed Planet" that serves as the epigraph reads, "Reason's a thing we dimly see in sleep." Power's view of

life as both unreason and sleep squares with the ontology
bodied forth by Plato's cave and Kant's noumenon: human
life, dealing with emanations of things and not things themselves, is unreal: reality exists beyond the scope of human
experience. Man's inability to know reality undergirds, as
well, the doctrine of original sin. Nor can this failure be im-
proved other than by divine grace, since our depravity rules
out the effectiveness of action. (The characters in the book
look ungainly and usually fail to carry out their aims when
they act.) The belief that human activity can be gainful
causes pride. Freedom, then, leads to sin. By acting, we violate the nature of things; we undermine social order, and we
rebel against God. *The Birds Fall Down* is Rebecca West's
fullest novelistic study of original sin. She plays it against
political history, she infuses it into personality, and she rubs
it into the skeletal system of her feminism: perhaps men
are more destructive than women because they are more
given to pragmatic action. What the epigraph foreshadows is
the folly of reason, or, to be more correct, what passes for
reason in human society. To adhere to a category of reason is
to subvert reason. One character, by applying Hegel's dialectic to his life, sparks a brushfire of violent acts that brings
about his own death and does not subside until the Bolshevik
revolution of 1917.

The novel's title also invokes Hegel. One character remi-
nisces about the bird hunts of his youth in Hegelian terms.
Part of the mating ritual of the cocks and hens involves leap-
ing into the air. The birds leap just before sex—the moment
when they are aflame with sexual passion. This, too, is the
moment the hunters fire their guns: "a system, perfect in
itself, and exquisitely ingenious, is destroyed at the very moment when it is implementing its perfection, by another system, just as perfect and ingenious." [38] Hegel saw life moving
forward by the clash of opposites. The opposition of the bird
hunt and the mating ritual shows passion murdered by intellect. *The Birds Fall Down* portrays love as a kind of death,
and it does not limit itself to sexual love. Death also infects
family love, political idealism, and religious fervor. In all
these cases, the cool and the studied defeat the spontaneous

and direct. The final step in this Hegelian march is the coming to power of Lenin, who was no bold extrovert but a wily infiltrator of organizations. Lenin's policy of subverting rather than overthrowing refers back to the bird hunt. Accordingly, the description of the hunt as a conflict of systems, and not as a drama of living beings, looks ahead to the growing impersonality of our century.

Rebecca West states the urgent need for new values by dotting her novel with numerous watches and clocks—most of which do not work. (One character's father is a watchmaker.) But then nothing seems to work as it should. Invertedness and irregularity have become ordinary, even admired. Laura Rowan remarks inwardly on her grandfather, "what she liked in him was the upside-downness of him." She then catches cold and another character gets a case of chilblains, even though the time is summer. In the same chapter, Laura notes another inversion: "her mother suddenly . . . [became] young and defenceless, even younger than she was herself." Even Laura's grandmother gets swept into the topsy-turviness: "There was royalty in reverse in her grandmother's shrunken body." [39] Nonrelatedness touches everything. The only daughter of a collapsing marriage, Laura is half Russian, half English; at eighteen, she straddles girlhood and womanhood; she is too old for school but too young to work; with her brothers away at school, she has nobody her age to talk to. Although she wants to grow up, she has no place in which to grow. The Russian revolutionaries are split into hostile camps. The Tsar, by exiling Laura's grandfather, the Count Nikolai Diakonov, has lost his most loyal follower. Now living in France, the country of liberal skepticism, Nikolai has lost touch with the country he has loved and served for many years. The rift between him and Russia is so deep-striking that it has torn him from himself: "His strength was evidently something apart from his health." [40]

As in Rebecca West's other work, the severing of a person from his native land always does harm in the novel. Internationalism means random dispersion. It destroys the vital flow between people and the forces that shaped them. The

Diakonovs' apartment in Paris has an Italian chest and a Persian rug; a cousin of the Count has married an American; the Count later hears about Russian terrorist cells in Lausanne, Paris, London, and Glasgow. Politically, this shapeless grey mass boils into the Bolshevik rising and the international Communist conspiracy that followed it. At the more personal level, all of the major characters end the novel in exile from their native countries. Rebecca West maintains comic distance by sending one of them, a Russian, to a school in England as a French teacher—under an assumed name and forged credentials submitted to a Belgian employment service.

The drama of discontinuity begins when Tania, nerve-worn over her marriage and her mother's health, decides to take Laura to Paris. Her parents' apartment, occupying the top floor of "the most somber building" [41] on the street, prefigures calamity with its dim lights and dark, heavily ribbed appointments. The heavy ikons, the ponderous furniture, and the outdated dress of the servants convey perfectly a ruined majesty. And matching the jaded opulence of the fourth-story eyrie is the man who lives there—Laura's exiled grandfather and the Tsar's former minister of justice, the Count Nikolai. His person, his philosophy, and the political system he stands for, like his residence, are all topheavy anachronisms. He embodies the rotten-ripe forces of dogma during a ferment of liberalism. He must be helped into chairs, he knocks off his secretary's eyeglasses, and he upsets a table while greeting his daughter and granddaughter. His banishment is the unhappy result of security lapses in high tsarist circles. Slippages in government security had been traced to him after his personal secretary, one Kamensky, secretly helped the terrorists kill several of the Tsar's best chiefs. Although innocent, Nikolai has accepted his banishment as he would any other decree of the Tsar. To Nikolai, the Tsar is infallible—a saint and a martyr; like Shakespeare's kings, he sacrifices morals to preserve the innocence of his subjects.

Nikolai's obedience bears out his faith in imperial order. He clings to his faith even though it cuts him off from the things he loves—the laws, the forms, the people of Russia. The scrappy, shadowy life offered by his apartment, the "poisoned air" of which has broken his wife, is all he has outside of memories: "He could not have set foot outside the apartment without being followed by a crowd." [42] Suitably, he dies the same day he takes a train to the Riviera. Seeking to arrest movement and progress, he cannot survive the experience of the moving train. He dies in a hotel, an epitome of homelessness. His apartness is complete. Death finds him "as much out of place in [a] coquettishly curtained bed as if he had been a horse or a bull," and he performs his own funeral rites.

One of the people tending him in his last sickness accidentally calls him "the Archduke." [43] Although literally false, the title does apply poetically. Like that of the Archduke Franz Ferdinand in Sarajevo in 1914, Nikolai's death ends an historical epoch. Rebecca West's attitude toward the Count is complex. On the one hand, he is cruel and selfish and neglectful of his family. His pious maunderings on the subject of Holy Russia and the resentment he harbors against Rome because of the Fourth Crusade get the full sting of Rebecca West's satire. On the other hand, his age, his gnarled, towering bulk, his contempt for personal danger, and his unshakable loyalty make him the only heroic figure in the book. This last descendent of a race of primitive Slavic giants ennobles the monarchist code by the honor and dignity of his commitment. Although outmoded, his massively held certainties generate a tragic depth. A character remarks somewhere that Nikolai, as a Slav, is no European. His ability to surrender himself to an experience, regardless of whether the experience is happy or sad, makes good the observation. His passionate engagement with life surpasses that of all the other characters in spite of his age and uprootedness.

The book's central incident is a train ride from Paris, during which Laura and Nikolai are surprised by one Vassili Iulievitch Chubinov, the son of one of Nikolai's oldest friends, a member of the minor Russian nobility, and now a terrorist spy. Chubinov tells Nikolai the reason for his banishment—once again, that Nikolai's personal secretary, Kamensky, stole information which allowed the terrorists to murder several of the Tsar's chief aides. Kamensky's betrayal is more than Nikolai can bear. He suffers an attack at Grissaint, in northern France and dies the same day, literally railroaded to his death. Chubinov is the same kind of mousy, nondescript destroyer found in Graham Greene and Alfred Hitchcock: "He was middle-sized, lean and pale, with unkempt hair and meagre beard and moustache, all mouse-brown, and grey eyes behind spectacles." [44] At the start of the long, stylized debate between the two men, the issues seem sharply defined—tradition, dogma, and monarchism opposing dissent, rationalism, and liberalism. Yet Rebecca West humanizes the debate, first, by making Nikolai the mentor and boyhood idol of Chubinov and, secondly, by showing that a revolutionary always contains in himself that which he aims to destroy.

Chubinov commits the typically male failing of trying to swathe himself in a set of abstractions. By denying emotion, he becomes emotion's fool. Instead of joining morals to reason, as he insists, he acts on impulse and sentiment. He cannot drive out his long-standing love for Nikolai or the social snobbery attending his noble birth. He quickly becomes brittle and defensive, hiding behind the stock creeds and slogans of the party battle cry. His shoddily reasoned and recklessly applied egalitarianism makes him as much of a dogmatist as Nikolai. To appreciate the Slavic mystique that pervades the two men and their political dialogue, it is best to go to an introduction Rebecca West wrote for a 1926 selection of Carl Sandburg's poems. Any nation or community locked in the middle of a vast continent will become introspective, the essay says. Although advances in communication have nullified her argument, Rebecca West argued in 1926 that Russia and the American Midwest of Sandburg's poems both tend to a "facile mysticism," a self-congratulatory blend of religion, politics, and mission. Divided from other cultures, the isolated nation or community acts as its own audience and measure of excellence. At best, this collective stock-taking makes for solid tradition; at worst, it promotes racism in the lowest sense. In either case, group morality is both rigid and pervasive. So whereas America's ethic of rugged individualism makes the rich man a national hero, Russia's feudal-agrarian tradition accords the same honor to the poor peasant.[45] Luba Couranoff, a Russian princess in *The Thinking Reed*, settles happily in St. Louis because, like Russia, Missouri lies on a vast inland plain.

Rebecca West views society as a massive, swaying folk rhythm neither rational in origin nor subject to the test of reason. She does not reject Nikolai's view of Russia as a featureless, monotonous beauty. The following description of Russia, by Nikolai, recalls a Chekhov short story: "There is no point where it begins and none where it ends, and every place seems its heart." [46] In practice, strict obedience to authority may offer as much access to being as liberal humanism. Nikolai uses the Russian Orthodox worship service to explain the all-encompassing love fostered by the dynastic principle:

> We Russians know that religion is for the moral and the immoral. It is the love of God for man meeting with the love of man for God, and God loves the vicious and the criminal and the idle as well as He loves the industrious and the honest and the truthful and the abstinent. He humbles himself to ask for the love of the murderer, the drunkard, the liar, the beggar, the thief. Only God can achieve this sublime and insane relationship.[47]

Chubinov could not parry this argument. But lest Nikolai feel morally superior, Chubinov reminds him that "There's no moral difference between us" and that "We're the children of the same dream." And although Nikolai never credits Chubinov for being anything but a criminal and an atheist, he does admit, when told of a problem within the terrorist ranks, "This often happens to us on our side of the fence." His later use of the Marxist catchphrase, the withering away of the state, establishes another sameness between the monarchist and the terrorist. The two men share the same avid interest in politics, they converse easily, they are betrayed by the same man, and they harbor the same guilt:

"Oh God," exclaimed Nikolai, "were you, the son of my friend, a party to all those crimes?"

"Why, so were you," said Chubinov.[48]

This sameness overrides politics and the law. Chubinov's dead wife and Nikolai's dying wife (not to mention Edward Rowan's spurned wife) show that the real clash of life-styles does not set authority against revolution but male absorption in public affairs against female rootedness in the home. Rebecca West rejects on emotional grounds Chubinov's program of upheaval. And although she approves Nikolai's theocratism emotionally, she rejects intellectually its refusal to accept change as a sign of healthy organic growth.

This moral issue is embedded in language. The outstanding feat of *The Birds Fall Down* is the book's power to bring home the Slavic spirit, i.e., Slavicness, through language. Differences between Nikolai and Chubinov do break down — but not by orderly, consecutive argument or sudden revelation of idea. Let us go back to the account of Chabrinovitch, an accomplice in the killing of the Archduke Franz Ferdinand in *Black Lamb and Grey Falcon*, to see the unique way Slavs match language to life:

> He took all experience that came his way and played with it, discussed it, overstated it, understated it, moaned over it, joked about it, tried out all its intellectual and emotional possibilities.[49]

The Birds Fall Down seizes upon this uniqueness and brings it to life. The Slavs in the book do not talk to report facts or ideas. Slavic conversation expresses selfhood. Dialogue in the familiar sense is barely present. Once a person starts to talk, he will continue at length. Interruptions, rejoinders, and leading questions are out of place. Speeches seldom answer each other; shouting, pleading, moralizing, and reminiscing, they aim less for precision than for engulfment. Whatever orderly progression of thought they contain is accidental. The mind tumbles from event to event and from association to association. Nor are Rebecca West's Slavs ignorant of the uses of their linguistic lavishings. To score a point, Kamensky buries the trim, precise Edward Rowan under an avalanche of words; Chubinov later outwits two French policemen with the same trick. When the Slav breaks down the denotative aspects of words and treats his subject as a tissue of spoken sounds, the western mind is lost.

The life-styles, philosophies, and speech habits of Nikolai and Chubinov meet in Kamensky. Linguist, engineer, and spy, Kamensky first strikes us with his smallness. The adjective, "little," describes him four times on the page where he is first named.[50] On the surface, it looks as if the biddable Kamensky wants nothing but to serve the Count. He can always be depended on to serve tea at the right time, to arrange the details of a trip, to take the Madame Diakonova to church. And indeed he loves doing these things. Yet behind the truckling modesty, he remains his own man. Always figuring, ever alert, he has raised himself by self-abasement. The "huge construction of lowliness"[51] he has built over the years has gained him the full trust of the Count. Kamensky's kind of destroyer, the Chaplinesque Judas, has its female counterpart in Edward Rowan's mistress, Susie Staunton. She, too, wins the day by pretending to be less important than she is. And she, too, as a close friend of Rowan's wife, Tania, subverts a personal trust. One feels these two destroyers chipping away at man's finest capabilities. Susie insults Tania's beauty as a fillip to stealing her husband, and Kamensky's betrayal of both Nikolai and Chubinov subverts friendship and order. The real setting of *The Birds Fall Down* is not Edwardian England or France, but the crumbling bedrock described in the most prophetic poem of our century, Yeats's "The Second Coming." Allusions in the novel to the fifth cow, "the unidentifiable person, the guest at the party whom nobody knows,"[52] create a vision of final judgment. But if the last go first, then we are all done for. The only saving grace is our unreadiness. One point the book repeats is the wide gulf separating God and man. Perhaps we need more scourging before we can approach God. If the leader is the fifth cow or Banquo's fourth murderer, or the mysterious third man, he is also the stranger on the road to Emmaus. Maybe we are already in a state of grace. The chipped, impersonal, upside-down character of modern life, while taming our blood, has also averted the drastic act that will kill us all at once.

The character of Kamensky is based on Yevno-Meyer Fishelevich Azef, leader of the strongest terrorist cell in Russia during the early years of our century. The discovery in 1908 that Azef was a tsarist agent broke the spirit of the revolutionaries and cleared a track for Lenin and the Bolsheviks. Although posterity knows little about Azef's motives, Rebecca West uses her knowledge of both spying and pre-1917 Russian politics to do a brilliant character portrait. She shows through Kamensky the flesh-and-blood equivalents of ideas. Mastered by an idea, Kamensky sees himself as beyond good and evil. He not only works for the tsarists and the terrorists; he also believes in both systems of government, contradictory though they may be. Like Chubinov, he has strong ties to the regime which gave him life. When he says of the Count, "He was the centre of my being," [53] he is speaking the truth. He embraces the opposing systems of government in order to found a new one. An engineer, he does not stop at directing the movements of the Diakonov family. He must control history, too. A builder of bridges, he sees himself as the bridge connecting the old and new centuries.

Ironically, Kamensky dies as soon as he stops thinking of himself as an idea. He has just accepted a supervisor's job with a French construction firm in South America, where he wants to marry and raise a family. But a spy can have no stable domestic life. The aliases spies use point up the brokenness of their lives. Kamensky-Gorin-Kaspar, like Chubinov-Baraton and even Ulyanov-Lenin, becomes too self-divided to enjoy wholeness. Kamensky dies with a bouquet of flowers covering his face. His faceless death, like the facelessness of his life, shows that, rather than occupying center stage, he has whipped himself out of life. His deadpan comedy act has scored beyond his hopes. Here is the unofficial police report of his death:

He was one of those men of mystery we sometimes find on our hands. . . . All the labels on his clothes had been

carefully unpicked, even the tailor's marks which custom-
ers don't usually know about had gone. . . . Handker-
chief of fine lawn, but no monogram. A silver cigarette
case, but no monogram. No papers of any sort, no
letters.[54]

An expert in hydraulics, Kamensky has the fluid personality
to work under pressure. Yet he must crack. A spy cannot
choose his assignment; nor can he resign when he wants. (It
must be noted that Kamensky's death may have been ordered by his chiefs to rule out the chance of his divulging
secret information.) The lot of a double agent is particularly
hard. *The New Meaning of Treason* explains how the self-
presence required by double agency is bound to twist the
double agent's personality:

> This is a dangerous game. The dyer's hand, as Shakespeare
> remarks, is subdued to what it works in. To pretend to be
> a traitor while practising an extreme form of loyalty is
> psychologically contortionist's work, and most people
> could no more do it than they can twist their legs round
> their necks.[55]

Although Kamensky stands as the keystone of one Hegelian drama, another is unfurling around him without his
knowledge. The building material of the bridges he uses to
connect the centuries is treachery. Betrayal is the fiber of
modern life. And not only are we all Judases; we single out
for betrayal the ones we love. The Tsar betrays Nikolai, his
faithful minister of justice. Nikolai, in turn, by setting politics above all else, betrays his dying wife. Edward Rowan, his
son-in-law, betrays both wife and daughter. The arch-Judas
is Kamensky. He betrays himself by doing double agency.
He loves Nikolai and bemoans his death with real tears but
does not regret betraying him. The reverence he holds for
Nikolai is matched by the reverence Chubinov feels for him.
Kamensky shows as clearly as anybody else in the book the
treacherous nature of love. Chubinov's words, along with his
later gunning-down of Kamensky-Gorin, bathe the drama in
a lurid glow. Despite our intentions, we are driven to murder
what we love:

I really will be helpless without Gorin. . . . My lifelong friend will kill me after I have killed him, and I won't care, for I love him too much to want to live after I have been his executioner.[56]

But Chubinov is just the instrument of Kamensky's death. Kamensky's Judas, the one who first arranges the murder and then hides the murder weapon, is Laura. Self-effacing, dishonest, and treacherous to love, she stands much closer to Kamensky than she knows: "It startled her that he lied so quickly and so well; as quickly as she had lied . . . a little while before, and rather better." [57] Laura is another who undersells herself in order to strengthen herself. Only her inexperience prevents her seeing that Kamensky has fallen in love with her. His belief, stated in his diary, that Laura returns his ardor, whereas she actually fears he will kill her, voices in another key the murderous nature of love and the loving nature of murder: we act alike to our lovers and our would-be killers. Laura's treachery may be worse for being unconscious. That an innocent girl can unknowingly kill the man who loves her suggests the indwelling treachery of us all. Her response to Kamensky's plans for marriage recoils sharply, not only on her, but on the rest of us, too: "What sort of woman would Kamensky love? Only a woman like himself, capable of treachery and murder." [58]

Everyone seems implicated in guilt. Edward Rowan is a leading statesman but fails as a husband and father. The other three male principals, Nikolai, Kamensky, and Chubinov, all serve elevated ideals; yet all three sanction violence. According to his own lights, Nikolai is deeply stained by evil. First, his carelessness puts restricted materials into Kamensky's hands. Next, Nikolai's coffin houses the pistol that killed Kamensky. In a punning mood, Rebecca West has the priest in charge of the funeral service place the packet with the gun in it against the soles of Nikolai's feet. Nikolai will lie forever with murder on his soul (soul-sole). Laura, who engineers all the steps of the engineer Kamensky's death save squeezing the trigger, universalizes the familiar theme of the contagion of power. *The Fountain Overflows* extended the notion of royal guilt by having Clare Aubrey break trust with her husband to protect her children. Laura's betrayal gets rid of the question of motives and responsibilities. All of us prey on each other simply to survive.

The corrupting force of power is not the only doctrine that the novel carries forward to a new development. The "lunatic" (the idea-ridden public man who neglects the persons and things closest him) reaches its zenith in Edward Rowan. Like Arnold Condorex of *Harriet Hume*, the spies in *The New Meaning of Treason*, and the three Russian public men in *The Birds Fall Down*, Rowan adds little to the world's store of happiness. His exertions question once again the force of human will: can our choices mean anything? are we free to know or save ourselves? The failures of the four males in the book answer these questions negatively. Men use politics as a way of having fun. Although they can stop playing any time, they seem driven to see the game through to its destructive end. Rowan's unconcern for Laura's welfare and his love affair with Susie Staunton grow logically out of his gamesmanship. A notable politician, he has already centered his life outside the home. Since a man's sexual needs rarely stay put when his public fortunes soar, it follows that Rowan should slant his erotic drives away from his wife. The bringing-forward of ideas and character types from her earlier books suggests that Rebecca West planned *The Birds Fall Down* as a final inventory of reality. The rising fortunes of Susie Staunton and Kamensky are not the book's only apocalyptic echoes. The servants preparing Nikolai's funeral dinner rouse Pentecostal meanings: "The Russians were talking Russian to the French, the French were talking French to the Russians, and although neither knew more than a few words of the other's language, the conversation was coherent." In *The Idea of A Christian Society*, T. S. Eliot said that religious fear must precede religious hope; in *The Court and the Castle*, Rebecca West spoke of "a healthy fear of destruction." [59] *The Birds Fall Down* is her attempt to restore a religious intensity to life.

The tragic mindlessness of the universe, the macabre humor, the low-keyed technique used to describe gripping events—these traits reaffirm Conrad as the novel's chief influence. Rebecca West even cadences her sentences like those of Conrad. The quoted passage reflects Conrad's practice of making the mental physical by following a description with a summary statement all the more jarring for its quiet economy: "When the light came back she [Laura] found that Kamensky was breathing deeply too, and in the same rhythm as herself. They were in horrid physical agreement." [60] The novel's Conradian strain also helps show how far Rebecca West has advanced as an artist. The artistic distance between Jenny Baldry, the passive narrator of *The Return of the Soldier*, and Laura Rowan spells out the extent of Rebecca West's growth. Jenny had no dramatic function. Laura is both active and integral aside from serving as the central intelligence of *The Birds Fall Down*. Unlike Jenny's, her point of view is not static. At first, her youth prevents her from understanding the things she sees and hears. But her later immersion in lies and betrayal matures her quickly. The shaping of her mind is exciting to watch. Sometimes, a new event will release the meaning of an earlier one. Certain things she knows subliminally; in these cases, she either will not or dares not trace a pattern of inferences. Often, a political event will clarify something in her parents' marriage. But always, her sex, her innocence, and her aristocratic background make her responses lucid and candid. Nikolai's opinion that she needs iron is wrong. She rises to the challenge of life even after she sees life springing from a moral death and the death of her secure past.

The book ends on a bitter note. In the next to last paragraph, Laura and her mother welcome the advent of the new century; technology and science, they agree, will insure happiness and prosperity for all. But the cream of the jest occurs in the ironical way Rebecca West matches her novel's subject matter to its form. That a description of breakdown and disorder should have a balanced, well-ordered form is the final Hegelian clash of *The Birds Fall Down*. But the opposing horns of order and disorder also serve as the forceps which bring the new century into life.

5

The Jubilee

The best way into *Black Lamb and Grey Falcon: A Journey through Yugoslavia* is through two contemporary reviews. *Time* called it "an omnibus record of her [Rebecca West's] journey—part travelogue, part history, part philosophical and political asides—one of the most passionate, eloquent, violent, beautifully written books of our time." Viewing it within the tradition of travel literature, Katherine Woods called it in the *New York Times Book Review* "the magnification and intensification of the travel book form," also "its apotheosis." [1] Unable in her four early novels to dramatize the full range of her imaginative powers, Rebecca West grounds her biggest and boldest work in Yugoslavian culture. It is a storehouse of recipes, dates, opinions, historical and geographical facts, and religious lore. Nor does it shrink from mixing the trivial and the profound. The book's attitude is one of comic acceptance; along with Diocletian and St. Augustine, it ranges Mae West, Al Capone, Walt Disney's Minnie and Mickey Mouse, and the brand names of many familiar household items. In fact, the most common subjects sometimes inspire her best writing:

> In their very triviality, these shops afforded delight. I never made a more agreeable purchase than a halfpenny cone of roasted nubs of sweet corn. The shop sold nothing else: they lay in great scented golden heaps, through which there ran a ghostly crepitance as soon as one grain was touched. The owner must have heard it a million million times; it still amused him. [2]

To convey her thronging subject matter, Rebecca West quotes documents and statistics, surveys historical epochs, takes excerpts from speeches, uses techniques of the thriller and silent-film comedy, and talks to Yugoslavians at random. The book has no rigid epistemology. Some of its richest material comes from scraps of conversation with people in trains, restaurants, and hotel lobbies. Irrigating this material is a basic liking for people; her candor in approaching people and her ability to listen to them brings out their best. Rebecca West is good company. Her zest for concrete physical experience and the "thinginess" of things sends her happily along the docks, marketplaces, and byroads of the Balkan peninsula. She reacts dramatically to setting; through the inhabitants, customs, and artifacts of a locale, she can capture its sensation. Sometimes she seizes upon a specific detail, like a woman's dress, and will note its material, cut, and embroidery. If she likes it, she will even try it on, as she does with the traditional Mostar garb of Herzegovina.

Incidents like these show her personality to be as far-ranging and many-sided as her subject matter. The book is full of charming personal asides and self-revelations. Balancing her commitment to pressing moral concerns is a bracing self-irony. She knows that life is too serious to be taken seriously all the time. So she makes fun of herself, includes playful anecdotes, and joins trivial conversations. Her openness allows her to view life from many angles; her literary skill allows her to discuss it in many voices. *Black Lamb and Grey Falcon* harbors some of her worst prose, but it also contains some of her best. Her scene-painting of the minarets, the huddled white houses, and the bright green poplars of Sarajevo shimmers with lyric vitality. Her ear is as keen as her eye. Its softly winding cadences and concluding words give the following sentence a Tennysonian quiet that is perfect:

On the edge of this cemetery, fringed with beds of purple iris, there runs a promenade from which a hillside of grass and fruit trees drops steeply to the Vardar river, winding silver among its golden poplars and willows.[3]

The versatility of Rebecca West's style creates many surprises. Because she can get at her subjects from so many different angles, she can uncover dramatic new possibilities. Although her vast learning makes for some of this excitement, the book also gathers both variety and weight through its deft use of repetition, understatement, metaphor, and paradox.

It is one thing to write about a sequence of events. It is another to shape a thousand years of Yugoslavian culture into an aesthetic whole. One way Rebecca West achieves unity is by stringing her 1180-page narrative around several historical events which occurred on St. Vitus's Day, 28 June. 28 June 1389 marked the first battle of Kossovo, where the Serbian army's loss to the Turks delivered Serbia into five hundred years of slavery. The event around which the first volume of *Black Lamb and Grey Falcon* turns also happened on St. Vitus's Day: the 1914 killing of the Archduke Franz Ferdinand, heir to the Habsburg throne, in Sarajevo, capital of Bosnia, near the Austro-Serbian frontier. Rebecca West's account of the events leading to the attentat, or royal murder, has the suspense of a 1930 thriller by Dorothy Sayers, Margery Allingham, or Agatha Christie. It captures first the political maneuvering in the Viennese court at the time, alternating straight historical narrative, dialogue, and time shift. The Archduke stands as firmly in the Habsburg tradition of cruelty and waste as the Serbs do in a tradition of bravery. His presence in Sarajevo in June 1914 typifies Habsburg grossness. St. Vitus's Day is a day of mourning for all Serbians, and no conqueror should pay a state visit on a defeated people on the anniversary of their worst defeat. The Archduke's favorite pastime, hunting, furnishes the metaphor that spells out the cold inevitability of his death, the metaphor of the battue:

> Franz Ferdinand's greatness as a hunter had depended not only on his pre-eminence as a shot, but on his power of organizing battues. He was specially proud of an improvement he had made in the hunting of hare: his beaters, placed in a pear-shaped formation, drove all the hares to-

wards him so that he was able without effort to exceed the
bag of all other guns. . . . The earth and sky were nar-
rowed . . . by the beaters to just one spot, the spot where
it must die; and so it was with this man. . . . If by some
miracle his slow-working and clumsy mind could have become swift and subtle, it could not have shown him a safe
road out of Sarajevo. Long ago he himself, and the blood
which was in his veins, had placed at their posts the beaters who should drive him down through a narrowing world
to the spot where Princip's bullet would find him.[4]

Rebecca West's portrait of the stuffed Archduke as the final
finished product of a century of Habsburg misrule is no cari-
cature. His butchery and misanthropy were well known before the writing of *Black Lamb and Grey Falcon*. His devotion as a husband and father had attracted less note. Yet
Rebecca West mentions his family loyalty several times and
includes it in her assessment of his character. Nor does she
weight the scales in favor of his Bosnian assassins. The clum-
siness, poor timing, and divided purposes of the conspirators
even shock her: "It might have been supposed that Franz
Ferdinand would never have been more safe than he would
be on St. Vitus's Day at Sarajevo." Both the mounting and
the carrying-out of the attentat rival the Archduke's conduct
in unreason. The compound passive verb and the tired
rhythm of the final sentence of the chapter describing the
attentat convey brilliantly the paralysis of the event: "At
last the bullets had been coaxed out of the reluctant revolver
to the bodies of the eager victims.[5]

The next chapter ("Sarajevo VI") describes the wild after-
math of the killing. The funeral arrangements and the political repercussions of the royal murder reflect the same
madness as the murder itself. The chapter ends as brilliantly
as the previous one; introduced in the last paragraph is a
poetic note that knits the many elements of the drama:

Only one person involved in this business did what he
meant to do: Princip believed he ought to kill Franz
Ferdinand, and he shot him dead. . . . The dead pair,
who had dreamed of empire stretching from the Baltic to

the Black Sea, surrendered the small primary power to breathe. . . . The conspirators wanted to throw their bombs, and could not. . . . There was an exquisite appropriateness in this common fate which fell on all those connected with the events of that St. Vitus's Day; for those who are victims of what is known as St. Vitus's disease suffer an uncontrollable disposition to involuntary motions.[6]

This strong metaphor does not close the investigation. Just when Rebecca West seems finished with the drama of St. Vitus's Day, 1914, she uncovers a rich new source of information. The first paragraph of the next chapter begins with the suggestion that she and her husband visit the graves of the young conspirators. In this chapter, she both moves personally closer to the attentat and uses the attentat as the basis of some new moral generalizations. After discussing the systematic destruction of Sarajevo's stores, prisons, and newspaper offices, she focuses on the imprisonment and trial of Princip, Chabrinovitch, and Grabezh. This phase of the drama repeats the same moral paralysis enacted elsewhere in the attentat. Not only were the prisoners mistreated and the trial mishandled. The authorities omitted the possibility of the trial's serving any civilized purpose whatever. Reason gave way to the battle cries of revenge. The unreason of the trial prevents our understanding it; and unless we understand an event, we have no way of learning enough from it to control its recurrence. Rebecca West's sober, measured tone imparts a fearsome inevitability to the savagery taking place in the courtroom:

The trial was for long veiled from common knowledge. Only certain highly official German and Austrian newspapers were allowed to send correspondents. . . . There were naturally no English or French correspondents . . . and there were apparently no American journalists. None could follow Serbo-Croat, so they took their material from their German colleagues. The most dramatic event of our time was thus completely hidden from us at the time when it most affected us.[7]

Rebecca West likes life to touch her directly. Unwilling to settle for a textbook encounter with the attentat, she goes to the places visited by the Archduke the day of his death, and she later meets the sister of the conspirator Chabrinovitch. Besides adding immediacy, this interview discloses new information. It makes public the danger faced by Chabrinovitch's family the day of the murder; it allows Rebecca West to see unpublished photographs of the murder; it gives her access to a French translation of the trial that lay forgotten in a filing cabinet nearly ten years.

The last section of Volume 1, "Serbia," like the one before it, "Bosnia," is historical-interpretive. But instead of fixing on one event and its outcroppings, like "Bosnia" did with Sarajevo 1914, it spans Balkan history from Napoleon's occupation to Mussolini's invasion of Dalmatia. These contrasting historical techniques add a pleasing variety, and the variety is further refreshed by the frame Rebecca West places around her two long historical sections. "Herzegovina," the short section preceding "Bosnia," is more symbolic than historical or realistic. Accordingly, the last chapter of "Serbia," which ends Volume 1, has a strong personal flavor. It reports the mood in Belgrade following the murder of the Yugoslavian king, Alexander, in Marseilles in 1934. It also establishes the importance of the character called Gerda, the German wife of the tour guide. Anti-Jew and anti-Slav, Gerda takes every opportunity to spoil the tour. Her most objectionable act is her decision to join the touring party on its trip to Macedonia. The Good Friday departure of the travelers signals pain before affirmation. What promised to be the zenith of Rebecca West's trip has chilled into an occasion of helpless anger:

> I stood transfixed with horror. Tears began to run down my cheeks. Macedonia was the most beautiful place that I had ever seen in my life, I had looked forward to showing it to my husband, and now we were to be accompanied by this disagreeable woman who liked neither of us. . . . And her contempt for everything Slav and non-German would be at its most peevish in Macedonia, which is the

most Slav part of Yugoslavia, and which is not only non-German but non-Occidental, being strongly Byzantine and even Asiatic.[8]

The volume ends as it started—on a moving train. The death of Tolstoy in a train station, the sealed train that carried Lenin to the Finland Station, the train ride that begins Ford's *Parade's End*, and the signing of the Armistice in a railway coach has made the train a symbol of transition between the old and new centuries. This legacy from the recent past explains why Rebecca West chose a moving train as the scene of her political debate in *The Birds Fall Down*. In *Black Lamb and Grey Falcon* it points elsewhere. The last page of the first volume shows Gerda snubbing Rebecca West's offer to sit next to the window. As the window stands for perception, clarity, and interchange, Gerda's rudeness goes beyond mere personal affront. Her rejection of the window dovetails with her racism to prepare thematically for the Nazi menace of Volume 2.

The second volume opens with a blast of hope. Gerda's rudeness has nearly annulled Easter. But joy peals forth in mighty waves when the travelers attend Easter services in an Orthodox church: "Suddenly, the full crash of the Easter ritual was upon us." [9] The flaming tapers, the thronging, plangent music, and the riot of colors scatter doubt and mistrust. But the gloom lifts only for a while. Following hope with despair and Christian ritual with pagan ritual, this first section of Volume 2 ("Macedonia") introduces and then explains the symbolic myth of the black lamb. The organization of the rest of the book can be easily charted. The next section ("Old Serbia") channels the black lamb into medieval Serbian history and then moves ahead to the ritual of the grey falcon—its origin and relevance to the Southern Slavs. The myths are combined and brought up to date in the next section ("Montenegro"), the last before the Epilogue. It must be noted that Rebecca West stays away from her two major symbols throughout the first volume; the title does not release its meaning until page 914. Aside from heightening reader interest, this delaying strategy builds power for her symbols. Slavic history knits so well with the two symbolic myths that, when they emerge, they do so with resounding authority. As in a Henry James novel, they represent that dramatic turn that forces us to reinterpret all that went before.

The relevance of the two myths is sharpened by technique: whereas the linchpin of the first volume of the book was an event—Sarajevo 1914—the second volume is held together by setting—the battlefield of Kossovo. This tragic setting commemorates the death of a civilization. The Serbian army was beaten by the Turks four times at Kossovo—in 1389, 1403, 1448–52, and 1831. The 1389 struggle, which may be the most important event in Serbian history and which took place on St. Vitus's Day, gets into both volumes of *Black Lamb and Grey Falcon*. In the first volume, Rebecca West visits the monastery of Vrdnik, where the Tsar Lazar, the defeated Serbian general, lies in state. The Tsar is the key figure in the myth of the grey falcon. The myth resembles the situation of the Fourth Tempter in Eliot's *Murder in the Cathedral*: a grey falcon, symbolizing St. Elijah, comes to the Tsar at Kossovo and asks him to choose between an earthly kingdom that will last but a short time and a heavenly kingdom that will last forever. By choosing the heavenly kingdom, the Tsar also chose death for himself and his soldiers and cleared a road to five hundred years of Islam rule. The myth has many meanings: self-betrayal, the sacrifice of the concrete to the abstract, the misconception that God requires suffering in exchange for blessings, and the prideful assumption that knowing God's will and achieving eternal bliss fall within the purview of human control. Rebecca West criticizes sharply the myth's endorsement of pacifism. Kossovo freed nobody from bloodshed, relieved no poverty, and failed to aid the cause of love. The martyrdom of Kossovo was empty and self-defeating. The only way to protect the works of reason and love and to safeguard civilization is to meet aggression and tyranny with force. The bad so outweighs the good in our world that the perpetuation of the good deserves our finest energies.

Rebecca West concedes the strength backing up the grey falcon's appeal to put by our weapons and give up the battle. This strength rests partly on the humanistic notion that man, a moral reasoning being, must avoid violence; that if he can only win prizes by resorting to violence, the prizes are not worth winning. The theistic appeal of the grey falcon strikes just as deeply: it claims that resigning oneself to God's will surpasses acting on one's own. Because divine grace cannot operate until the battle is renounced, the only Christian choice is that of surrender. Rebecca West answers these arguments historically. So long as nations invade other nations in order to rob and kill their inhabitants, man must defend what he owns and loves. The failure of the radical left to accept this principle has raised the more tough-minded radical right to political power. In the meantime, civilization has been undermined. The speed and unpredictability of social change mean that the law usually lags behind existing conditions. By refusing to campaign and legislate vigorously, the radical left loses its creative role of bringing the law up to date. The emergence of the radical right as the major dissenting voice in government will stop social progress. Instead of insuring stability, this brake to civilized process will foment disorder. To narrow the gap between organic social change and an unchanging set of laws, the archconservative will impose a police state. His government will recruit the worst sort of sadistic roughnecks; their criminal instincts whetted, these public officials will steal the property of their countrymen, wipe out all political opposition, and then, having destroyed the orderly processes of their own civilization, go on to attack others.

The book's black and grey symbolism and its many examples of man's intrinsic malignity make for a chafing experience. The following extracts typify the author's bleak attitude toward mankind:

There is no use denying the horrible nature of our human destiny.

Man is a hating rather than a loving animal.

The quality of Balkan history, and indeed of all history, is disgusting.[10]

But evil has not engulfed all. There has always been a struggling emergence of joy and hope. The points of light flashing over the grey-black human landscape glint most brightly in Yugloslavia. The difference between the Western European and the Slavic life-styles occurs most dramatically in the Eastern Orthodox worship service. The robust hymns and lavish colors bespeak a healthy intensity which corrects the Puritan belief that good things may only be bought by pain. Western morality has become so enthralled with the disagreeable that it has raised pain to a moral category. It lacks the bravery, self-confidence, and exuberance that makes the Orthodox worship service such an avalanche of adoration. Unlike that of the timid West, the Slavic attitude toward life is additive: One improves life by adding good things to it, not by subtracting or bartering:

> The worshippers in Western countries come before the altar with the desire to subtract from the godhead and themselves; to subtract from the godhead by prayer, to subtract their dangerous adult qualities by affecting childishness. The worshippers at Shestine [in Croatia] had come before the altar with a habit of addition, which made them pour out the gift of their adoration on the godhead. . . . The effect had been of enormous, reassuring natural wealth.[11]

Slavic courage has kept liberty alive in Europe despite centuries of plunder by Venice, the Habsburgs, the Romanoffs, the Ottoman Empire, and, most recently, the Axis powers. Nowhere in European military policy has man's suicidal streak left such a stain as in the Balkans. A strong nation of southern Slavs would protect Europe against invasion, both from the East and the South. And the Balkans, although not strong, provided just that bulwark. For their service they have been poorly recompensed. Even though they saved western civilization from the Mongol and the Turk, the western powers, instead of rewarding them, have raided their lands, denied their right to self-government, and helped their oppressors. And the madness that gave rise to this treachery is still in force. Western ingratitude to the

Balkans did as much to start the Second World War as it did the First. The Treaty of London, drafted in 1915 to encourage Italy to join the Allies, promised Italy some land along the Balkan slopes of the Adriatic. Although the treaty was later annulled, Rebecca West feels that it roused Italian territorial greed. Referring to the Croatian victory over the Turks in 1683, which kept Europe from being Islamized, she expresses a personal debt to the southern Slavs:

> These people of Dalmatia gave the bread out of their mouths to save us of Western Europe from Islam. . . . The West has done much that is ill, it is vulgar and superficial and economically sadist; but it has not known that death in life which was suffered by the Christian provinces under the Ottoman Empire. From this the people of Rab had saved me: I should say, are saving me.[12]

The present-tense verb in the last sentence is no accident. Included in the Epilogue to *Black Lamb and Grey Falcon* is a tribute to Yugoslavia's campaign against Hitler. Not only did the Belgrade government choose heroically in defying Germany, since resistance to a stronger military force means sure defeat. By opting for destruction over submission, it forced a delay in Germany's battle plans, which gave England and Russia a chance to mobilize.

Yugoslavian bravery also defies the morality engendered by the myth of the black lamb. Suitably, Rebecca West waits until after the Nazi-prototype Gerda leaves the touring party before exploiting the myth. The black lamb is a greater threat than Gerda because, whereas Gerda denied tradition, the black lamb stands within tradition. Its point of origin is the fertility ritual of the Cowherd's Rock on the Sheep's Field in Macedonia, where a pagan priest cuts the throat of a black lamb. Rebecca West's first description of the setting captures the ugliness of both the rock and the ritual:

> It was a flat-topped rock, uneven in shape . . . and it was red-brown and gleaming, for it was entirely covered with the blood of the beasts that had been sacrificed on it during the night. . . . The spectacle was extremely disgust-

ing. The colour of spilt blood is not properly a colour, it is in itself discoloured, it is a visible display of putrescence. . . . A great many jars had been thrown down from the rock and lay in shards among the cocks' heads on the trodden grass.

The rock is not the work of chance. Rebecca West speaks of its "enormous authority" and its "added loathesomeness of familiarity." [13] Embedded in western psychology, literature, politics, and religion, it gets its strength from man's self-destructive urge. Our preference for sorrow, sterility, and death has lifted blood sacrifice to the level of holiness. The ritual violates reason on all counts. To assume that God exchanges blessings for bloodshed is to deny fertility. Murder goes against the maternal instinct: goodness and increase do not flow from cruelty: broken jars, cocks' heads, and the spilled blood of slaughtered lambs add nothing to the act of copulation. The sacrifice of the innocent lamb points up our worst traits—our tendency to give rein to our sadistic drives and our ability to accept oversimplified and dishonest explanations for the presence of evil.

The refusal to be responsible and mature, the notion that life is only obtainable by death, and man's addiction to the disagreeable create a moral vacuum for the totalitarian state. Like its nineteenth-century antecedent, imperialism, the fascist state commits the fault of extending its power beyond its range of control. The dictator's scorn for process disqualifies him from conducting process. Immediate gain becomes the mainspring of his party's program; since he does not know that conquering a nation and ruling a nation have little in common, he commits himself to a policy of waste. Hitler's ascendancy is the classic example of the cancellation of process in government. He became dictator of Germany without binding himself to the contractual duties of leadership, and, by raising a large army, generated a militarism that sought outlets in foreign conquest. England, on the other hand, took the sacrificial role bodied forth by Kossovo and the Cowherd's Rock. Although war with Germany was imminent, Chamberlain and his cabinet ministers took no steps to defend their country. And they would have remained inert if not for the thunder reverberating from the Balkans.

The epilogue contrasts British inertia with Yugoslavian élan. The shift to present-tense verbs in the following passage reaffirms Yugoslavia's heroic role as the defender of Western Europe:

> At dawn on April the sixth [1941] German planes raided Belgrade and continued the attack for four days. . . . Eight hundred planes flew low over the city and methodically destroyed the Palace, the university, the hospitals, the churches, the schools, and most of the dwelling-houses. Twenty-four thousand corpses were taken away to the cemeteries, and many others lie buried under the ruins. . . . From everywhere came the Germans and the Austrians. . . . The Italians shamelessly appeared in Dalmatia and Croatia, where by themselves they had never dared to go. . . . The Yugoslavian Army never capitulated . . . and the last remnants of it are still fighting, hidden in the mountains and forests.[14]

The epilogue ends with a reference to Alexander, the slain king whose murder in Marseilles in 1934 opened the book. The circular pattern of the book, the dead king, and the guerrilla action along Yugoslavia's mountains and forests augur rebirth. Accompanying this rebirth are others. Rebecca West, who began her two-volume work as a hospital patient, has given up her bed, gone to Yugoslavia, and written *Black Lamb and Grey Falcon*. Meanwhile, the Yugoslavian federation has come into being. Rebecca West describes Balkan hegemony as a dramatic poem the Balkan people are creating with their bodies as well as with their minds. What occupies her most interested speculations is whether the Belgrade government can blend creatively the different strains that make up the Balkan complex: Serbs, Dalmatians, Croats, Bosnians, Montenegrins, and Slovenes; Moslems and Christians; social practices deriving from Byzantium, Austro-Hungary, and Russia. Although she says a good deal about racial traits, Rebecca West is no racist. One of Yugoslavia's chief attractions, in fact, is its heterogeneity: "It's precisely because there are so many different peoples that Yugoslavia is so interesting. So many of these people have remarkable qualities, and it is fascinating to see whether they can be organized into an orderly state." [15]

As has been suggested, the most exciting things about Rebecca West's Easter journey do not appear on any travel agenda. Her love of the accidental, the unsponsored, and the contingent can be seen in her going to Yugoslavia to begin with. Yugoslavia, the place where Asia and Europe meet, fails to make sense by Anglo-American standards; the word, "Balkan," in fact, has become synonymous in the West with "peasant" or "pig farmer." Yet Rebecca West looks for beauty instead of ugliness and is richly rewarded. She not only grants Yugoslavia its uniqueness; she exults in it. There is something of the self-detachment of the mystic in her openness to the Yugoslavian experience. She reads Balkan history, joins native dances, attends religious services, sleeps in a Macedonian monastery, and rolls in Macedonian clover. This immersion in life outside herself shortens the distance between her personal fortunes and the fortunes of Europe at large. In brief, by immersing herself in Yugoslavia, she steps into history. She and her husband meet a Nazi spy in Petch posing as a Danish salesman of farm machinery: in Podgoritsa, they see Altdorff, "the chief German agent in Yugoslavia." [16] The last thing the touring party does before disbanding is to swim on a Dalmatian beach. But the affirmation suggested by the community swim is blunted. Assembled on the same beach with Rebecca West and her companions are the Italian diplomats who have just set the groundwork for Mussolini's Albanian campaign. The book ends on this sour, undercutting note, and Rebecca West reacts to the coming invasion as to a personal crisis.

Often, the coming together of a public and a private event suggests, if not universal guilt, then complicity in the century's malaise. Nor does the writer detach herself from this background of suffering. Visiting the reception room of Sarajevo's town hall, where the Archduke made his last public appearance, she is told by the tour guide, "Yes, he stood just where you are standing, and he too put his arm on the balustrade." [17] Other parallels occur more subtly; like Rebecca West's hospital vigil coinciding, first in time with the death of King Alexander, and, more roughly, in setting with the shooting of the Archduke, which took place on the way to another hospital.

Personalizing history is but one way she tightens narrative structure. She also brings Yugoslavia closer to the reader by aligning herself with other English travelers to the Balkans. Invoked several times are Miss Muir Mackenzie and Miss Irby, who visited the peninsula in the nineteenth century and wrote *Travels in the Slavonic Provinces of Turkey and Europe* (1867). The greatest of all English travelers, John Ruskin, is praised both directly and indirectly. In addition to noting Ruskin's service of bringing Italian painting to England, Rebecca West often uses a Ruskinian style to describe natural scenery. English, Scottish, and American references also clarify Yugoslavia for the English-speaking reader who has never visited the Balkans. This method of conveying the unknown by the known occurs first in the epigraph, where Rebecca West quotes the speech in *Henry* V where Fluellen likens Macedonia to Monmouth. Later, Bosnia recalls Jane Austen's Bath, and a Macedonian abbot is said to have "the *expertise* of Tammany about him." [18] Sometimes, the comparison is more thematic. She organizes a long historical survey of medieval Serbian history by means of a running parallel between the fourteenth-century Serbian monarch, King Milutin, and England's Henry VIII; both men share the qualities of lechery, political opportunism, and murderousness. Yet, when the comparison breaks down, it favors the Slav over the Saxon. English royalty outdoes its Serbian counterparts in evil:

> It is to be noted . . . that there is nothing in Milutin's reign comparable to the beheading of Anne Boleyn and Catherine Howard. In certain respects Milutin was far more civilized than Henry VIII, though he lived a hundred and fifty years earlier in a country that had been Christianized three hundred years later. . . . We know also what happened to Sir Thomas More; better luck at-

tended the Archbishop Jacob, who was fearless in his opposition to Milutin's tortuous matrimonial policy; yet
lost neither his life nor his archiepiscopate.[19]

The handling of space and time is still another technique
that makes Yugoslavia more vivid to the reader. The technique is the Hegelian one of explaining the whole by the
part. The practice of interpreting events as paradigms, em-
blems, or as symbols of larger events has a strong unifying
effect. The effect is all the stronger for relating to material
the reader is not familiar with. Speaking of the murder of
Alexander Obrenovitch, King of Serbia, and his wife Draga
in Belgrade in 1903, Rebecca West says, "When Alexander
and Draga fell . . . the whole of the modern world fell
with them." Consequently, Western Europe's contempt for
everything Balkan found perfect expression thirty-one years
later in the car King Alexander was riding at the time he was
killed:

> It is an old-fashioned vehicle—seven years old in 1934 and
> clumsily refitted with new coachwork after a smash—
> which had actually been used for the transport of better-
> class criminals. The French chauffeur is known to have
> protested against being made to drive a king in such an old
> piece of iron. It is right that the automobile should be in
> Belgrade, for it beautifully symbolizes the way the West-
> ern powers have dealt with the Balkans.

Places, as well as personalities and events, can stand as focal
points of large, complex dramas. An example is Sveti Naum,
a Macedonian monastary: "This is one of the places in the
world which . . . have a symbolic meaning. The existence
of such places is one of the determining factors in history." [20]

Rebecca West reworks time in a slightly different way—
but again for the twin purposes of unity and clarity. The
combined experiences of her Easter visit to the Balkans
hardly justify an 1180-page book. By using a time sequence
governed by theme and free association, she extends her
range of inclusiveness far beyond that offered by a straight
linear approach. The telescoping of personal experience,

contemporary politics, and medieval lore create exciting opportunities for comparative study. It also conveys the sensation of the oneness of history. This combined impression of unity, variety, and interrelatedness will often emerge from what looks like a digression. These "digressive" passages follow their own logic. A person, a work of art, or a stretch of scenery will start a series of associations. The associations tumble and glide into each other in such fresh ways that they annihilate chronological time. We read fifty, even a hundred, pages before learning that only minutes have elapsed. Either Rebecca West is rising from a meal she sat down to a short while before, or she is turning away from the statue or building which inspired the sequence of ideas she has been stringing together these many pages.

This coursing back and forth over long stretches of time, the many characters, the battle scenes, the ritual sacrifices, the trip to the underworld of a Serbian mine shaft, the founding of a new world order, and Balkan heroism over the centuries—this data makes *Black Lamb and Grey Falcon* a modern epic. Tallying with the epic design are the twelve sections, excluding map, bibliography, and index, that comprise the work. The mention of King Alexander's murder in the prologue sets forward its epical theme: the murder of royalty. Nor is Rebecca West unmindful of recent experiments with the epic. Her epilogue, a treatise on European unrest from 1934–41, recalls Tolstoy's two documentary epilogues to *War and Peace*. The mention of Ulysses on the prologue's first page, the interplay of micro- and macrocosm, and the various rhetorical techniques pressed into service—poetry, journalism, history, biography, personal reminiscence, dialogue—turn the mind to Joyce just as the psychological technique of free association recalls Proust. But Rebecca West does not borrow when she can innovate. Although many of the effects of Tolstoy, Joyce, and Proust lie beyond her powers, her alert use of contemporary materials makes *Black Lamb and Grey Falcon* an epic of our time.

The use of language and lore of different cultures, like the emphasis given to ritual, strikes resemblances with Frazer, Jung, Eliot, and the ecumenical spirit of today. Another contemporary motif is the moving train. Besides its above-mentioned cultural relevance as a transition-marker between centuries, the moving train was a popular device of film directors in the 1930s and 1940s (*The Lady Vanishes, Night Train, Brief Encounter*). By showing herself in the prologue aboard a Yugoslavia-bound train, Rebecca West provides something both exciting and familiar to spur reader interest. A sudden shift in setting on this first page introduces another modern symbol – the hospital. Her stay in the hospital labels Rebecca West as a victim of the age. The things she recalls best about her hospital vigil include reading a newspaper report and then hearing a radio broadcast of King Alexander's murder. She cannot escape the attentat. Shortly after her recovery, she sees a film of the attentat and says of the dying king, "he is as I was after the anaesthetic." [21] The reference to Eliot's *Prufrock* is clear enough. As has been mentioned, though, Alexander's death may have helped bring our drugged, supine world back to life. It did infuse Rebecca West with a harsh dose of reality. As Yugoslavia was a center of spying and internal unrest in the mid-1930s, her going there then took her to one of the most dangerous places in a continent moving toward danger.

Rebecca West, then, planned her trip to Yugoslavia as both an exploration of her age and a self-exploration. One reason the trip proves such a creative challenge is the presence of her husband. As a banker, Henry Andrews has at his command information that complements her theoretical-humanistic knowledge. As the man she has pledged herself to love, he is essential to her. Her twin explorations – of herself and her age – could not take place without him. The open, generous, loving friendship that emerges between husband and wife both vindicates and dignifies Rebecca West's philosophy. For her learning is anchored in love. She and her husband talk playfully and profoundly about many subjects. The freely shifting tone and level of their conversations stem from a long-standing mutual compassion. At other times, she describes herself losing an argument to him; she praises him ("My husband . . . an exceedingly polite man") and blames herself for mistreating him ("I complained, as wives should not"); she even tells a joke against herself concerning him:

> My husband sighed, and said. . . "Now in all my life I have never got on a train and met a woman I used to love. . . . It seems to me that the proper place for the beloved is the terminus, not the train." "I am, however, travelling with you on this occasion," I reminded him. "Yes, my dear, so you are," he said, closing his eyes.[22]

Instead of competing for the reader's admiration, she credits most of the book's best insights to him. The longest and most powerful disquisition in the book, a brilliant setting-forth of the doctrine of process, is spoken by him. At the same time, she does not consult him on every decision; nor does she ask the reader to share her high opinion of him. So little is clutching and forced in the Andrews' relationship, in fact, that *Black Lamb and Grey Falcon*, in addition to its other services, could do duty as a marriage manual.

The last paragraph of the bibliographical note ending the book is a handsome, loving tribute to Henry Andrews. It has a reassuring ring. That a person so dedicated to love should love so well sends out to all of us fresh rays of Easter sunshine and hope:

> As for my husband, Henry Andrews, it is true that whatever is best in this book is his, and that during the years of its writing he never flagged in his desire to relieve me of all the drudgery he could take on his shoulders. . . . It took great faith, for which I am most grateful.[23]

Notes

1 — The Wheel

1. Rebecca West, "Rudyard Kipling," in V. S. Pritchett, ed., *Turnstile One: A Literary Miscellany from the New Statesman and Nation* (London, 1948), p. 3; Rebecca West, *St. Augustine* (Edinburgh, 1933), p. 112.

2. Rebecca West, *Black Lamb and Grey Falcon: A Journey through Yugoslavia* (New York, 1967), p. 1084.

3. Rebecca West, "Curious Idolatry," *Ending in Earnest: A Literary Log* (Garden City, 1931), p. 177; Rebecca West, *A Letter to a Grandfather* (London, 1933), p. 10.

4. Rebecca West, "Elizabeth Montagu (1720–1800)," in Bonamy Dobrée, ed., *From Anne to Victoria* (London, 1937), p. 167.

5. West, *Black Lamb and Grey Falcon*, p. 81.

6. Patrick Braybrooke, "Rebecca West," *Novelists We Are Seven* (Philadelphia, 1926), p. 150.

7. Rebecca West, "Woman as Artist and Thinker," in Samuel D. Schmalhausen, ed., *Woman's Coming of Age: A Symposium* (New York, 1931), p. 379.

8. Rebecca West, "The Tribunal That Stirred England: Part 2," *Harper's*, 198, July 1949, p. 47.

9. G[eorge]. E[velyn]. Hutchinson, "The Dome," *The Itinerant Ivory Tower: Scientific and Literary Essays* (New Haven, 1953), p. 248.

10. West, *Black Lamb and Grey Falcon*, p. 382.

11. Rebecca West, "The Strange Necessity," *The Strange Necessity: Essays and Reviews* (London, 1928), p. 43; Rebecca West, *The Thinking Reed* (New York, 1936), pp. 231, 343.

12. Braybrooke, "Rebecca West," p. 142.

13. West, *Black Lamb and Grey Falcon*, p. 678.

14. Ibid., p. 3.

15. Rebecca West, *Harriet Hume: A London Fantasy* (London, 1929), p. 203; Rebecca West, "Charlotte Brontë: 1816–1855," in H. J. and Hugh Massingham, eds., *The Great Victorians* (London, 1932), p. 52.

16. Rebecca West, "Mrs. Pankhurst," *The Post Victorians*, introd., W. R. Inge (London, 1933), p. 484.

17. West, "Rudyard Kipling," p. 7.

18. West, "Journey's End," *Ending in Earnest*, pp. 49–50; "Evelyn Waugh," *Ending in Earnest*, p. 222.

19. West, *The Thinking Reed*, p. 133.

20. West, "The Long Chain of Criticism," *The Strange Necessity*, p. 259.

21. Rebecca West, *Henry James* (London, 1916), pp. 61–62.

22. West, *Black Lamb and Grey Falcon*, p. 903.

23. West, *The Thinking Reed*, p. 72.

24. Ibid., p. 289.

25. Ibid., p. 88; West, "The Strange Necessity," p. 31.

26. West, "The Strange Necessity," p. 13.

27. West, *Black Lamb and Grey Falcon*, p. 9.

28. West, "The Tribunal That Stirred England: Part 2," p. 49.

29. Rebecca West, "Tradition in Criticism," *"Tradition and Experiment in Present-Day Literature* (London, 1929), p. 194; Rebecca West, "Miss West, Mr. Eliot, and Mr. Parsons," *The Spectator*, 15 October 1932, p. 480.

30. West, "Battlefield and Sky," *The Strange Necessity*, pp. 291–301.

31. West, *Henry James*, pp. 52–53.

32. [David] Low and "Lynx," "John Galsworthy," *Lions and Lambs* (London, 1928), p. 144.

33. West, "Charlotte Brontë," p. 52.

34. Low and "Lynx," "Lloyd George," *Lions and Lambs*, p. 99.

35. West, "O. M.," *Ending in Earnest*, p. 131; "Evelyn Waugh," *Ending in Earnest*, p. 219; *Black Lamb and Grey Falcon*, p. 265.

36. West, "The Strange Necessity," p. 90.

37. Rebecca West, *Arnold Bennett Himself* (New York, 1931), pp. 6, 12.

38. West, "Battlefield and Sky," p. 298; "The Strange Necessity," p. 120.

39. West, *Henry James*, pp. 17, 64–65; "Regretfully," *Ending*

in Earnest, p. 282; " 'Journey's End' Again," *Ending in Earnest,* p. 77.

40. West, "The Strange Necessity," p. 83.

41. Hutchinson, "The Dome," p. 249.

42. Rebecca West, *The Court and the Castle: Some Treatments of a Recurrent Theme* (New Haven, 1957), pp. 5–6.

43. West, "Prizes and Handicaps," *Ending in Earnest,* p. 90.

44. West, "The Strange Necessity," p. 86.

45. Ibid., p. 168.

46. Rebecca West, "Goodness Doesn't Just Happen," in Edward P. Morgan, ed., *This I Believe: The Living Philosophies of One Hundred Thoughtful Men and Women in All Walks of Life—as Written for and with a Forward by Edward R. Murrow* (New York, 1952), p. 188.

47. West, "Charlotte Brontë," p. 57; "Mrs. Pankhurst," p. 480; Rebecca West, "Snobbery," in Hugh Kingsmill, ed., *The English Genius: A Survey of the English Achievement and Character* (London, 1938), p. 221.

48. West, *Black Lamb and Grey Falcon,* pp. 155, 637.

49. West, *The Court and the Castle,* p. 135.

50. Rebecca West, "The Tribunal That Stirred England: Part 1," *Harper's,* 198, June 1949, p. 22.

51. West, "Snobbery," p. 222.

52. Hutchinson, "The Dome," p. 244.

53. West, *St. Augustine,* p. 68.

54. "Land of Sacrifice: Beauty and Terror in Serbia: An English Writer's Explorations," *TLS,* 28 February 1942, p. 102.

55. West, *Black Lamb and Grey Falcon,* p. 868.

56. West, "The Strange Necessity," p. 52.

2—The Groove

1. Rebecca West, *The Thinking Reed* (New York, 1936), p. 356.

2. Rebecca West, "Lucky Boy," *The World's Best Short Stories of 1930: Sixteen Stories Selected by the Editors of Leading American Magazines,* with a Foreword by Paul Palmer (New York, 1930), p. 25.

3. Rebecca West, *The Return of the Soldier* (Garden City, 1918), pp. 25, 26.

4. Ibid., p. 42.

5. Frank Swinnerton, *The Georgian Scene* (New York, 1934), p. 388.

6. West, *The Return of the Soldier*, p. 118.

7. Ibid., p. 35.

8. Joseph Collins, "Two Literary Ladies of London: Katherine Mansfield and Rebecca West," *The Doctor Looks at Literature* (New York, 1923), p. 170; Walter Allen, *The Modern Novel* (New York, 1964), p. 62.

9. Collins, "Two Literary Ladies of London," p. 179.

10. Rebecca West, *The Judge* (New York, 1922), pp. 31, 82.

11. Ibid., p. 31.

12. Ibid., p. 30.

13. Ibid., p. 125.

14. Ibid., p. 180.

15. Ibid., p. 139.

16. Ibid., p. 204.

17. Ibid., p. 103.

18. Ibid., p. 148.

19. Ibid., pp. 46–47.

20. Patrick Braybrooke, "Rebecca West," *Novelists We Are Seven* (Philadelphia, 1926), p. 145.

21. Rebecca West, "Gide," *Ending in Earnest: A Literary Log* (Garden City, 1931), p. 191.

22. Rebecca West, *Harriet Hume: A London Fantasy* (London, 1929), pp. 108–9.

23. G[eorge]. E[velyn]. Hutchinson, "The Dome," *The Itinerant Ivory Tower: Scientific and Literary Essays* (New Haven, 1953), pp. 243, 246.

24. West, *Harriet Hume*, pp. 55–56.

25. Rebecca West, *A Letter to a Grandfather* (London, 1933), p. 12.

26. West, *Harriet Hume*, pp. 48, 113.

27. Joseph Warren Beach, *The Twentieth Century Novel: Studies in Technique* (New York, 1932), p. 494.

28. Rebecca West, *Black Lamb and Grey Falcon: A Journey through Yugoslavia* (New York, 1967), p. 1084.

29. West, *The Thinking Reed*, p. 134.

30. Ibid., pp. 3, 4, 127.

31. Rebecca West, *Henry James* (London, 1916), p. 70.

32. West, *The Thinking Reed*, p. 19.

33. Ibid., p. 195.

34. Ibid., p. 89.

35. Ibid., p. 30.

36. West, *Black Lamb and Grey Falcon*, pp. 827–28; West, *The Thinking Reed*, pp. 30, 35.

37. West, *The Thinking Reed*, pp. 66, 257, 311.

38. Ibid., p. 221.
39. Ibid., p. 284.
40. Ibid., p. 314.
41. Ibid., pp. 128, 142.
42. Ibid.
43. Ibid., pp. 103–4, 311.
44. Ibid., pp. 58–59, 178, 179.
45. Ibid., p. 126.

3—The Court

1. As in *Black Lamb and Grey Falcon*, Rebecca West is sometimes careless with dates in *The Court and the Castle*; for instance, she gives 1880 as the publication of Henry James's book on Hawthorne and 1875 as the publication date of James's "first book": Rebecca West, *The Court and the Castle. Some Treatments of a Recurrent Theme* (New Haven, 1957), pp. 203–4.
2. West, *The Court and the Castle*, p. 8.
3. Ibid., p. 17.
4. Ibid., pp. 22, 23, 25, 245.
5. Ibid., pp. 121, 125, 211.
6. Ibid., p. 56.
7. Ibid., p. 4.
8. Ibid., p. 38.
9. Ibid., p. 70.
10. Ibid., pp. 114–15.
11. Ibid., p. 130.
12. Ibid., p. 141.
13. Ibid., p. 288.
14. Cecil Beaton and Kenneth Tynan, *Persona Grata* (New York, 1954), p. 95.
15. Rebecca West, *A Train of Powder* (New York, 1955), pp. 215, 275.
16. Rebecca West, "Goodness Doesn't Just Happen," in Edward P. Morgan, ed., *This I Believe: The Living Philosophies of One Hundred Thoughtful Men and Women in All Walks of Life—as Written for and with a Foreword by Edward R. Murrow* (New York, 1952), p. 187.
17. West, *A Train of Powder*, pp. 10, 143, 144, 261, 279.
18. Ibid., p. 238.
19. Ibid., pp. 75, 165.
20. Ibid., p. 3.
21. Ibid., p. 37.

22. Ibid., p. 5.

23. Ibid., p. 46.

24. Ibid., p. 165.

25. Ibid., p. 76.

26. Ibid., p. 81.

27. Ibid., p. 93.

28. Ibid., p. 99.

29. Ibid., p. 168.

30. Ibid., p. 207.

31. Ibid., p. 213.

32. Ibid., p. 214.

33. Ibid., pp. 218–19.

34. Ibid., p. 224.

35. Ibid., pp. 269–70.

36 Ibid., p. 290.

37. Ibid., p. 310.

38. Rebecca West, *The New Meaning of Treason* (New York, 1964), p. 29.

39. Ibid., p. 12.

40. Rebecca West, *A Letter to a Grandfather* (London, 1933), p. 33.

41. West, *The New Meaning of Treason*, p. 183.

42. Ibid., pp. 188, 191.

43. Ibid., p. 205.

44. Ibid., p. 212.

45. Ibid., p. 216.

46. Ibid., p. 264.

47. Ibid., pp. 338, 341.

48. Ibid., pp. 4, 5, 157, 192, 244.

49. Rebecca West, "The Englishman Abroad," in Ernest Baker, ed., *The Character of England* (Oxford, 1947), p. 503.

50. Margret Boveri, *Treason in the Twentieth Century*, trans., Jonathan Steinberg (London, 1961), p. 13.

51. West, *The New Meaning of Treason*, pp. 54, 290.

52. Beaton and Tynan, *Persona Grata*, pp. 95–96.

53. West, *The New Meaning of Treason*, pp. 202, 280.

54. Ibid., pp. 317–18.

4–The Comet

1. W. Somerset Maugham, *The Summing Up*, with a foreward by Glenway Wescott (New York, 1964), p. 52.

2. Rebecca West, *The Court and the Castle: Some Treatments of a Recurrent Theme* (New Haven, 1957), p. 52.

3. "Circles of Perdition," *Time*, 8 December 1947, p. 118.

4. Rebecca West, *Black Lamb and Grey Falcon: A Journey through Yugoslavia* (New York, 1967), pp. 196, 337, 616; Rebecca West, *The New Meaning of Treason* (New York, 1964), p. 209; Rebecca West, *A Train of Powder* (New York, 1955), p. 118.

5. West, *Black Lamb and Grey Falcon*, p. 820; *The New Meaning of Treason*, p. 45.

6. West, *A Train of Powder*, p. 286; *The New Meaning of Treason*, p. 270.

7. Bernard Kalb, "The Author," *Saturday Review of Literature*, 19 March 1955, p. 13; John K. Hutchens, "Rebecca West, Novelist and Great Reporter," *New York Herald Tribune Book Review*, 22 April 1956, p. 2; for the biographical background of *The Fountain Overflows*, see Rebecca West, "A Visit to a Godmother," in Norman Nicholson et al., *Writers on Themselves* (London, 1964), pp. 8–16.

8. Harvey Curtis Webster, "A Visit with Rebecca West," *Saturday Review*, 8 December 1956, p. 14.

9. Elizabeth Janeway, "It All Happens Within the Family," *New York Times Book Review*, 9 December 1956, p. 1.

10. Rebecca West, *The Fountain Overflows* (New York, 1956), p. 15.

11. Ibid., p. 301.

12. Ibid., p. 67.

13. Ibid., p. 290.

14. Ibid., pp. 52, 55.

15. Ibid., p. 276.

16. Ibid., pp. 151–52.

17. Ibid., p. 174.

18. Ibid., p. 421.

19. Webster, "A Visit with Rebecca West," p. 14. (The trilogy will not materialize. In a personal interview [September 1970] Dame Rebecca told the writer of the present book that she plans no sequels to *The Fountain Overflows*.)

20. James Gray, "SR's Book of the Week: 'The Fountain Overflows,' Author: Rebecca West," *Saturday Review*, 8 December 1956, p. 14; Janeway, "It All Happens Within the Family," p. 1.

21. West, *The Fountain Overflows*, pp. 6, 44, 408.

22. Ibid., p. 131.

23. Ibid., p. 403.

24. See Note 8, above.

25. West, *The Fountain Overflows*, p. 298.

26. Ibid., p. 289.

27. Ibid., p. 64.

28. West, *The New Meaning of Treason*, p. 47.

29. West, *The Fountain Overflows*, p. 125.

30. Rebecca West, "Goodness Doesn't Just Happen," in Edward P. Morgan, ed., *This I Believe: The Living Philosophies of One Hundred Thoughtful Men and Women in All Walks of Life—as Written for and with a Foreword by Edward R. Murrow* (New York, 1952), p. 371.

31. West, *The Fountain Overflows*, p. 255.

32. Ibid., pp. 15, 46, 56, 65.

33. Ibid., pp. 433–35.

34. Rebecca West, *The Birds Fall Down* (New York, 1966), p. 9.

35. Ibid., p. 366.

36. Ibid., p. 20.

37. Dame Rebecca West, "The Event and Its Image," in Peter Green, ed., *Essays by Divers Hands: Being the Transactions of the Royal Society of Literature*, new series, 31 (London, 1962), p. 187; West, *The Birds Fall Down*, pp. 391, 392.

38. West, *The Birds Fall Down*, p. 76.

39. Ibid., pp. 16, 55.

40. Ibid., p. 231.

41. Ibid., p. 14.

42. Ibid., pp. 15, 21.

43. Ibid., pp. 241, 283.

44. Ibid., p. 91.

45. Carl Sandburg, *Selected Poems of Carl Sandburg*, ed. and with an introduction by Rebecca West (New York, [1926] 1954), p. 23.

46. West, *The Birds Fall Down*, p. 71.

47. Ibid., pp. 61–62.

48. Ibid., pp. 101, 109, 115, 120, 260.

49. West, *Black Lamb and Grey Falcon*, p. 379.

50. West, *The Birds Fall Down*, p. 11.

51. Ibid., p. 11.

52. Ibid., p. 330.

53. Ibid., p. 298.

54. Ibid., pp. 411–12.

55. West, *The New Meaning of Treason*, p. 305.

56. West, *The Birds Fall Down*, p. 205.

57. Ibid., pp. 41–42.

58. Ibid., p. 429.

59. Ibid., p. 422; West, *The Court and the Castle*, p. 94.

60. West, *The Birds Fall Down*, p. 352.

5—The Jubilee

1. "Heaven and Earth in the Balkans," *Time*, 11 November 1941, p. 94; Katherine Woods, "Rebecca West's Brilliant Mosaic of Yugoslavian Travel, *New York Times Book Review*, 26 October 1941, p. 4.

2. Rebecca West, *Black Lamb and Grey Falcon: A Journey through Yugoslavia* (New York, 1967), p. 648.

3. Ibid., p. 659.

4. Ibid., p. 336.

5. Ibid., pp. 360–61.

6. Ibid., p. 370.

7. Ibid., p. 374.

8. Ibid., pp. 623–24.

9. Ibid., p. 636.

10. Ibid., pp. 148, 302, 488.

11. Ibid., p. 81.

12. Ibid., p. 137.

13. Ibid., pp. 823, 827.

14. Ibid., pp. 1146–47.

15. Ibid., p. 662.

16. Ibid., p. 1028.

17. Ibid., p. 333.

18. Ibid., pp. 461, 702.

19. Ibid., p. 854.

20. Ibid., pp. 11, 471, 746.

21. Ibid., p. 16.

22. Ibid., pp. 764, 457.

23. Ibid., p. 1158.

Selected Bibliography

This list includes only those items on Rebecca West which seem to me especially interesting. Titles of exceptional import are marked with an asterisk.

Allen, Walter. *The Modern Novel.* New York, 1964, pp. 62–64.

Beach, Joseph Warren. *The Twentieth Century Novel: Studies in Technique.* New York, 1932, pp. 493–95.

Braybrooke, Patrick. "Rebecca West." *Novelists We Are Seven.* Philadelphia, 1926, pp. 141–56.

Collins, Joseph. "Two Literary Ladies of London: Katherine Mansfield and Rebecca West." *The Doctor Looks at Literature.* New York, 1923, pp. 151–80, esp. pp. 169–80.

Davis, Herbert. "The New Writers: 18: Rebecca West." *Canadian Forum,* June 1931, pp. 340–41.

* Hutchinson, G[eorge]. E[velyn]. "The Dome." *The Itinerant Ivory Tower: Scientific and Literary Essays.* New Haven, 1953, pp. 241–55.

* ———. *A Preliminary List of the Writings of Rebecca West: 1912–1951.* New Haven, 1957.

Overton, Grant. "Rebecca West: An Artist." *When Winter Comes to Main Street.* New York, 1922, pp. 78–87.

"Rebecca West: Twentieth Century Woman." *MD: Medical Newsmagazine,* vol. 14, no. 10, October 1970, pp. 191–96.

Index

"Abel, Colonel," 90–91, 96
Addison, Joseph, 26
Adler, Alfred, 45
Alexander, King of Yugoslavia: murder of in 1934 in Marseilles; 135, 142–47 passim
Allen, Walter: on *The Return of the Soldier*, 34
Altdorff, 143
Amis, Kingsley: *The Anti-Death League*, 114
Anatomy of a Murder, 68
Andrews, Henry, husband of Rebecca West, 147–48
Aristotle, 26
Auden, W. H.: poems based on T. E. Lawrence, 39; mentioned, 47
Augustine, St.: influence on *The Judge*, 37–38; named the shaping force of western literature, 61; influence on *The Fountain Overflows*, 104; mentioned, 1–4 passim, 28, 82, 130
Austen, Jane, 20, 65, 144
Azef, Yevno-Meyer Fishelevich: a character in *The Birds Fall Down* modeled on him, 125

Beach, Joseph Warren: *The Twentieth Century Novel*,

35; mentioned, 46
Beethoven, Ludwig von, 22, 23
Bennett, Arnold: *The Old Wives' Tale*, 22, 113; mentioned, 2, 22
Berry, James, 72, 74
Blake, William: supplies epigraph of *The Fountain Overflows*, 100
Boleyn, Anne, 144
Bookman, The, 12
Boveri, Margret: *Treason in the Twentieth Century*, 92
Braybrooke, Patrick: criticism of *The Judge*, 41–42; mentioned, 5, 9
Brief Encounter (film), 147
British Union of Fascists, 28, 92, 99
Brontë, Charlotte, 10, 21, 27
Brontë, Emily: *Wuthering Heights*, 40; mentioned, 30
Burgess, Anthony: *Tremor of Intent*, 114
Burgess, Guy, 89–90 passim

Calvin, John, 1
Capone, Al, 130
Carlyle, Thomas, 70
Cézanne, Paul, 23
Chabrinovitch, conspirator in the murder of Archduke

161